CONSCIENTIOUS OBJECTIONS

ALSO BY NEIL POSTMAN

Technopoly

Amusing Ourselves to Death

The Disappearance of Childhood

Teaching as a Conserving Activity

Crazy Talk, Stupid Talk

Teaching as a Subversive Activity
(with Charles Weingartner)

CONSCIENTIOUS OBJECTIONS

Stirring Up Trouble About
Language, Technology,
and Education

NEIL POSTMAN

VINTAGE BOOKS
A DIVISION OF RANDOM HOUSE, INC.
NEW YORK

FIRST VINTAGE BOOKS EDITION, FEBRUARY 1992

"Megatons for Anthromegs" was originally published in
The Village Voice. Reprinted by permission of *The Village Voice*.
Grateful acknowledgment is made to *Saturday Review* for
permission to reprint "Etiquette" by Neil Postman on page 6
(The Phoenix Nest) of *Saturday Review*, June 8, 1963.
Copyright © 1963 by *Saturday Review*.
Reprinted by permission.

Additional acknowledgments of previous publication of
selections contained in the present work, and of permission to
reprint such previously published material, will be found in the
Acknowledgments on p. ix.

Library of Congress Cataloging-in-Publication Data
Postman, Neil.
Conscientious objections : stirring up trouble about language,
technology, and education / Neil Postman. — 1st Vintage Books ed.
p.   cm.
Originally published: 1st ed. New York : Knopf, 1988.
Includes index.
ISBN 0-679-73421-X
1. Language and education.   2. Technology—Social aspects.
3. Mass media—United States.   I. Title.
[P40.8.P667   1992]
303.4'0973—dc20   91-58082
CIP

Manufactured in the United States of America
10 9 8 7 6 5

To my parents

CONTENTS

ACKNOWLEDGMENTS

Some of the essays in this book appeared in various journals, although in significantly different forms. "Social Science as Moral Theology" made its debut as a speech and then appeared in *Et Cetera*. "The Naming of Missiles" began its journey to these pages as a much shorter piece in *The Realist*. "My German Question," as noted in the preface to the piece, appeared in *Stern* in German; it has not been published in English before. "A Muted Celebration" was commissioned by the New York University alumni magazine but makes its first published appearance here. "The Parable of the Ring Around the Collar" appeared in a lengthier version in *Panorama*. "Etiquette" appeared in the *Saturday Review* and is reprinted by permission. "Megatons for Anthromegs" appeared in a somewhat different form in *The Village Voice* and is also reprinted by permission. "Safe-Fail," an experiment which *Liberation* took a chance on, appears here as a more well-developed story.

The essay entitled "The News" is the product of a collaboration with Professor Jay Rosen of New York University, and any of its inadequacies are his, not mine: which is to say, he has given me permission to include that last remark. He is one of several colleagues and students on whom I have inflicted my ideas and whose generosity of spirit has encouraged me to put them forward in this book.

PREFACE

The two best places for a writer to live are America and Russia. Both are dynamic imperial powers prone to making mistakes. I should not like to live in Switzerland. Switzerland does not make mistakes, and therefore deprives a writer of grievances. For a writer, that society is best which is most burdensome. The favor is returned: for a society, that writer is best who is most burdensome.

It is true enough that in Russia writers with serious grievances are arrested, while in America they are merely featured on television talk shows where all that is arrested is their development. This is an important difference, but it does nothing to change the fact that grievance is the source of all interesting prose. Without grievance, a writer tends to become a celebrant, which is an agreeable but repetitious state. After you have sung two choruses of "God Bless America," what else is there to say?

I must hasten to add that though grievance is a necessary condition for good prose, it is far from sufficient. There are, after all, differences between a writer and a wimp. The differences are easier to notice than to describe, but we may at least say this: a good writer is a wimp who has found a unique and prudent form in which to say "No." I use the word "unique" to mean that the form is well suited to the nature of the writer, assuming the writer is sane. I use the word "prudent" to mean that the form is well suited to the nature of the grievance, assuming the grievance is sane. According to these definitions, there is no better complaint ever written than the Declaration of Independence or a worse one than *Mein Kampf*. Among writers whose exposition, by my lights, has achieved triumphs of nay-saying are George Orwell, who found his form in a humorless, crystalline understatement; H. L. Mencken, who found his in a brassy, mean-spirited, but imaginative sarcasm; and Russell Baker, who finds his in detached whimsy. My impression is that today Orwell is read very little, and then only in school, Mencken not at all. This is a sorrowful condition, with ominous overtones for the well-being of the Republic. Fortunately, Baker is available and inexhaustible. I imagine him to be like some fourth-century citizen of Rome who is amused and intrigued by the Empire's collapse but who still cares enough to mock the stupidities that are hastening its end. He is, in my opinion, a precious national resource, and as long as he does not get his own television show, America will remain stronger than Russia.

It is possible that the essays included here will earn no judgment higher than wimpery recollected in tranquillity. Readers, as always, will decide. But they are entitled to know at the start what I intend. There is a theme to these essays, or, to be exact, three themes that make a single whole; that is to say, I think of them as inseparable. Together, they have formed the core of my academic interests for thirty years.

First, some of the essays are about the triumphs of one-eyed technology and, in particular, how these triumphs have laid waste some of our most creative, not to mention charming, habits of thought. I call technology one-eyed because, like Cyclops, it sees only what is directly in front of it. I am not, let it be said, some latter-day Luddite. I raise no complaint against a machine doing what it was designed to do. After all, who expects a machine to notice its own side effects? To care about the social and psychic consequences of its own presence? Machines ask no questions, have no peripheral vision or depth perception. They see the future through the fixed eye of their technical possibilities. But it is well said that in the country of the blind, the one-eyed man is king. In America, and increasingly in Europe, technology is a one-eyed king ruling unopposed amidst idiot cheering. I object to this state of affairs, and I would like some of my essays to lend support to lively discussions of where we are being taken, and in whose interests, by the unfettered development of technology. It is clear enough that our engineers, not our poets, are the unacknowledged legislators of our time, and perhaps that is as it should be. But unless there is a vigorous opposition party, technological tyranny is inevitable. Man cannot live by electric wiring alone, and this obvious fact must be part of any plans we make for the future.

A second theme in these essays may be placed under the heading "the humiliation of the word"—which, of course, has everything to do with the first theme. The phrase is taken from one of Jacques Ellul's books, and I use it here because it is both a provocative and an accurate metaphor for one of the more distressing consequences of what Ellul calls the technological society: that the power, utility, and prestige of the word have been significantly diminished. Ellul attributes this decline to the rise and omnipresence of visual forms of communication—not only film and video technology but also posters, billboards, cartoons, art reproductions, photography, and, of course, advertising in all its manifestations.

Ellul's complaint is essentially the same one made by Daniel Boorstin in his famous book of a quarter of a century ago, *The Image*. And it was made even before that by Rudolph Arnheim in his book *Film as Art*. Others have worried just as much about the humiliation of the word. Harold Innis, for example, in one of his last essays, "A Plea for Time," argued that the speed, range, and impersonality of modern media undermine the oral tradition and therefore weaken the possibility of a nourishing community life. And in these days when lying is called misspeaking or disinformation, one cannot forget George Orwell, who concluded that in the age of advertising and public relations, Newspeak becomes the normal mode of discourse.

Indeed, for forty years a conversation has taken place among our most prescient social critics about the alarming decline of both the spoken and the written word as instruments of civilized discourse. Some of my essays are intended to contribute to that conversation, although with perhaps less optimism than I can usually muster. I am constrained by the thought that the decline of language may have proceeded so far that most people no longer perceive it as a problem. An analogy here might clarify what I mean. It is said that the brain is the only organ of our body that feels no pain and therefore does not know when it is injured. The brain does not regard brain damage as a problem. If we think of language as the brain of a civilization, then it is possible that severe language-damage may not be perceived by the social body as a problem. It is possible that we have adapted ourselves to disinformation, to Newspeak, to public-relations hype, to imagery disguised as thought, to picture newspapers and magazines, to religion revealed in the form of entertainment, to politics in the form of a thirty-second television commercial. In adapting ourselves, we come to accept the present situation as the only available standard, and conclude with Dr. Pangloss that this is the best of all possible worlds.

But perhaps this is not the case. There does appear to be a national concern about illiteracy, aliteracy, and the persisting decline in our young people's analytic ability. There is even a movement—as I write—that wants to give the highest priority to teaching critical thinking in the schools.

Which leads to the third theme of these essays, education, a subject never far from the issues raised by technology and language. By my reckoning, the three most traumatic conflicts in Western education occurred, first, in the fifth century B.C., when Athens was undergoing a change from an oral culture to an alphabet-writing culture; second, the sixteenth century A.D., when Europe underwent a radical transformation as a result of the printing press; and third, now, in the late twentieth century, as a result of the electronic revolution, particularly the invention of television. It has been wisely said by the great historian of American education Lawrence Cremin that whenever America needs a revolution, it gets a new school curriculum. He meant to suggest that our schools are always the focal point of our attempts to understand and resolve new conditions of culture. The subject of education is vibrant and filled with challenge precisely because no one knows what it should be like in our own times. We are safe in assuming only that what we are presently doing is wrong—an irresistible situation for a complainer.

There are three last points in need of mention. First, some of the essays were composed to be spoken, and I have let them remain in that form. After several attempts to make them more hospitable to a conventional standard of exposition, I had to acknowledge that the discipline required in directing one's remarks to a specific audience enforced an economy of expression that was too easily lost if one tampered with the text.

Second, a brief prologue to each essay (or, in some cases,

to a brace of essays) explains the circumstances or the question that produced it, the context that gave life to my grievance. I know the essays must stand or fall on their own merits, but the Jewish mother in me made me think that a word or two about their pedigree might get them off to a good start.

Finally, among the several synonyms for the word "conscientious" is the word "dutiful." That is the meaning I mostly had in mind in choosing the book's title. Sometimes it is great fun to complain and, in America, it can even be profitable. But unless one's complaints are grounded in a sense of duty to one's country or to a recognizable humane tradition, they are not worthy of serious attention.

Therefore, I write as a devoted patriot who wishes to celebrate the best by noticing the worst. Readers must decide if I have found a unique and prudent form in which to do this.

CONSCIENTIOUS OBJECTIONS

Social Science as Moral Theology

I begin with this essay because it provides the reader with the frame within which I compose my conscientious objections. I see myself as a storyteller (non-fiction division), make no claims to being a scientist, am not insulted when my essays are called polemical. Indeed, as I hope to make clear, there is a measure of cultural self-delusion in the prevalent belief that psychologists, sociologists, anthropologists, and other moral theologians are doing something different from storytelling. The New York Times could help if it stopped reporting their work on its Science Page. It could help even more if it added a Moral Theology Page to which "social scientists" of every variety (including economists) could regularly contribute.

Without getting misty-eyed about it, I think we can fairly say that universities have a sacred responsibility to define for their society what is worthwhile knowledge. These definitions are most clearly visible in university catalogues, where you will find lists of courses, subjects, and "fields" of study. Taken together, they amount to a certified statement of what the university thinks a serious student ought to think about. In what is omitted from a catalogue, you may also learn what a serious student need not think about.

This observation is in no way a criticism of universities. You cannot have a university which does not, in some way, organize learning and by so doing attribute relative value to categories of knowledge. The trouble is that sometimes a university can suffer from hardening of the categories. This happens when certified scholars resolve, against all reason, to defend their customary view of knowledge from encroachment by more novel perspectives. Why scholars should fall into this state of mind is, all by itself, a fascinating issue and probably should be included in university catalogues as a course, or a subject, or even a field of study. Abraham Maslow devoted a portion of his career to studying the matter, and in his book *The Psychology of Science* he concluded that science (and by extension, scholarship generally) can be "a safety philosophy, a security system, a complicated way of avoiding anxiety and upsetting problems. . . . It can become—in the hands of some people, at least—a social institution with primarily defensive, conserving functions, ordering and stabilizing rather than discovering and renewing." Maslow went on to describe in some detail the psychopathology of scholarship which when given its head almost always leads to an environment of extreme intellectual sterility. Of course it must be said, and Maslow said it, that when it is not psychopathic, the conserving impulse in scholarship is quite important, since it serves to protect an intellectual community from expending energy on trivial and even depraved categories of knowledge such as elocution and astrology.

But these are bad times for scrupulous efforts at gatekeeping, and, happily, many universities are now busily engaged in rewriting their catalogues. A pervasive and lively energy, especially in our great universities, is being directed toward the expansion of categories, models, and theories, toward the development of new subjects. Among the most prominent of these is the subject known variously as "Communication," or "Media Studies," or (as we call it at my university) "Media Ecology." This takes as its domain the study of the cultural consequences of media change: how media affect our forms of social organization, our cognitive habits, and our political ideas. As a young subject, media ecology must address such fundamental questions as how to define "media," where to look for cultural change, and how to link changes in our media environment with changes in our ways of behaving and feeling. But such questions rest on another, larger question which is as yet unanswered— namely, what kind of subject is this to be? Is it a science? Is it a branch of philosophy? Is it a form of social criticism? Where, in short, do we place it in the catalogue?

The usual, indeed the only, answer is that the subject must be a social science. Therefore, in this essay I will address two fundamental questions: What are legitimate forms of research in the social sciences? And, what are the purposes of conducting such research?

I must say at the start that I reject the implications of the phrase "social science." I do not believe psychologists, sociologists, anthropologists, *or* media ecologists do science, and Michael Oakeshott's distinction between processes and practices is definitive in explaining why. Oakeshott means by processes those events that occur in nature, such as the orbiting of planets or the melting of ice or the production of chlorophyll in a leaf. Such processes have nothing to do with human intelligence, are governed by immutable laws, and are, so to say, determined by the structure of nature. If one were so inclined, one might even say that processes are the creation of God. By practices, on the other hand, Oakeshott means the creations of people—those events that result from human decisions and actions, such as this essay or the formation of a new government or our conversations at dinner or falling in love. These events are a function of human intelligence interacting with environment, and although, to be sure, there is a measure of regularity in human affairs, such affairs are not determined by immutable laws. Now, I have been told by friendly colleagues that this last statement, namely, that human actions are not determined by immutable and universal laws, cannot be proved, and that to assert it is in the nature of a metaphysical speculation. Fair enough. You may consider it, then, to be part of my metaphysics that I believe in free will and in choice; that human beings are fundamentally different from orbiting planets and melting ice; and that while we are profoundly influenced by our environment, our ideas and behavior are not irrevocably determined by natural laws, immutable or otherwise. In other words, I believe with Oakeshott that there is an irrevocable difference between a blink and a wink. A blink can be classified as a process, meaning it has physiological causes which can be understood and explained within the context of established postulates and theories; but a wink must be classified as a practice, filled with personal and to some extent unknowable meanings and, in any case, quite impossible to explain or predict in terms of causal relations.

As I understand it, science is the quest to find the immutable and universal laws that govern processes, and does so on the assumption that there are cause-and-effect relations among these processes. In this definition, I place myself, even if only beside their feet, with Newton and the last of the great Newtonians, Albert Einstein. It follows that I believe the quest to understand human behavior and feeling can in no sense except the most trivial be called science. The trivial-minded point, of course, to the fact that students of natural law and human behavior both often quantify their observations, and on this common ground may be classified together. A fair analogy would be to argue that since a house painter and an artist both use paint, they are engaged in the same enterprise, and to the same end.

The scientist uses mathematics to assist in uncovering and describing the structure of nature. At best, the sociologist (to take one example) uses quantification merely to give some precision to his ideas. But there is nothing especially scientific in that. All sorts of people count things in order to achieve precision without claiming that they are scientists. Detectives and bail bondsmen count the number of murders committed in their city; judges count the number of divorce actions in their jurisdictions; business executives count the amount of money spent in their stores; and young children like to count their toes and fingers in order not to be vague about how many they have. Information of this kind may sometimes be valuable in helping a person get an idea, or, even more so, in providing support for an idea. Numbers may even be useful in browbeating people into accepting an idea that otherwise has no merit. I have, myself, harbored several such worthless ideas, one of which has recently been supplied with some impressive numbers that not only will permit me to continue to believe this nonsense, but may help me to persuade others to believe it. I refer to my theory that living in California, Florida, and other warm climates tends to shrivel the brain and makes people dumber than those living in colder climates, such as New York, Pennsylvania, Illinois, and Iowa. Since there is no idea so bad that a social scientist will not find support for it, I was not surprised to come across a study by two doctoral students at Texas Technical University who found that the ten states with the highest average SAT scores all had cold winters. Indeed, *every* state with an average of 510 or higher on both the verbal and quantitative parts of the SAT had an average high temperature in January of less than 42 degrees Fahrenheit. At the other end, five of the ten states with the lowest SAT scores were warm-weather states. Moreover, temperature had a significant relationship to SAT scores even when the researchers took into account such factors as per-pupil expenditures on schooling. So there!

Just as counting things does not a scientist make, neither does observing things, though it is sometimes said that if one is empirical, one is scientific. To be empirical means to look at things before drawing conclusions. Everyone, therefore, is an empiricist, with the possible exception of paranoid schizophrenics. To be empirical also means to offer evidence that others can see as clearly as you. You may, for example, conclude that I like to write essays, offering as evidence that I have written this one and that there are several others contained in this book. You may also offer as evidence a tape recording, which I will gladly supply, on which I tell you that I like to write essays. Such evidence may be said to be empirical, and your conclusion empirically based. But you are not therefore acting as a scientist. You are acting as a rational person, to which condition many people who are not scientists may make a just claim.

Some time ago, I had a conversation with a young communications professor from a midwestern university who repeatedly claimed to be a member of the community of social scientists. The basis of her claim was that she had conducted what is called a correlational study of television viewing and aggressive behavior in children, the conclusion of which was that some children in the state capital who watch lots of violent programs are also apt to act more aggressively than some of the children who watch fewer violent programs. She could not say—and had no hope of saying—whether they were aggressive because they watched television violence, or watched television violence because they were aggressive. She could also not say—and had no aspiration to say—why it was that some children who watched many violent programs did not act aggressively, or why some of those who didn't watch violent programs did act aggressively. Moreover, she told me that within the past five years there have been more than 2,500 such studies conducted in American universities, with the result that there is no agreement on very much except that watching violent television programs *may* be a contributing factor in making *some* children act aggressively, but that in any case it is not entirely clear what constitutes aggressive behavior. In other words, after 2,500 studies, we have a statement that is somewhat less meaningful than my saying that Ronald Reagan's telegenic charm may have been a contributing factor to his being elected President.

Confronted by such a desiccated view of science, I naturally asked what her definition of science was. She replied that it required one to be empirical, to measure things, to make one's methods and conclusions public, and to test one's assertions. Because this definition would not distinguish the act of science from the normal working of a sane mind engaged in problem-solving, it did not take me long to get her to acknowledge that such actions, while necessary in science, were hardly sufficient, and I was able to reduce her to saying, "Well, what difference does it make what you call it?" Now, this is not normally the way one ought to treat a young professor, but I did so because I believe it is important to distinguish science from non-science.

There are three reasons why. First, it is always worthwhile to insist that people explain the words they have chosen to describe what they are doing, so that their purposes may be evaluated. Second, many people who use the word "science" do so in the hope that its prestige will attach to their work. Americans are peculiarly afflicted with science-adoration, which is why we must endure such abominations as the oxymorons Christian Science, Creation Science, Scientology, Policy Science, Decision Science, and Administrative Science, as well as Behavioral and Social Science. And third, when the study of human conduct is classified as science, there is a tendency to limit the kinds of inquiries that may be made: counters and "empiricists"—that is, pseudo-scientists—are apt to deprive others of the right to proceed in alternative ways, for example, by denying them tenure. The result is, of course, that they impoverish all of us and make it difficult for people with ideas to be heard.

I want to give one more example of social science to make clear why I would not call it science at all. A piece of work that is greatly admired as social science, at least from a technical if not an ethical point of view, is the set of experiments (so called) supervised by Stanley Milgram, the account of which was published under the title *Obedience to Authority*. In this notorious study, Milgram sought to entice people to give electric shocks to "innocent victims" who were in fact conspirators in the experiment and did not actually receive the shocks. Nonetheless, most of Milgram's subjects *believed* that the victims were receiving the shocks, and many of them, under pressure, gave shocks that, were they real, might have killed the victim. Milgram took great care in designing the environment in which all this took place, and his book is filled with statistics that indicate how many did or did not do what the experimenters told them to do. As I recall, somewhere in the neighborhood of 65 percent of his subjects were rather more compliant than would have been good for the health of their victims. Milgram drew the following conclusion from his research: In the face of what they construe to be legitimate authority, most people will do what they are told. Or, to put it another way, the social context in which people find themselves will be a controlling factor in how they behave.

Now, in the first place, this conclusion is merely a commonplace of human experience, known by just about everyone from Maimonides to my Aunt Molly. The exceptions seem to be American psychiatrists. Before he conducted his experiment, Milgram sent to a large group of psychiatrists a questionnaire in which he solicited their opinions as to how many subjects would be likely to continue giving electric shocks when ordered to do so. The psychiatrists thought the number would be very much smaller than it actually was, basing their estimates on their knowledge of human behavior. Which explains to my complete satisfaction why their estimates were so wrong. I do not mean to imply that real scientists never produce commonplaces, but only that it is rare, and never a cause for excitement. On the other hand, commonplace conclusions are almost always a characteristic of academic pseudo-science.

In the second place, Milgram's study is not empirical in the strict sense, since it is not based on observations of people in natural life situations. I assume that no one is especially interested in how people behave in a laboratory at Yale or any other university; what matters is how people behave in situations where their behavior makes a difference to their lives. But any conclusions that can be drawn from Milgram's study must specify that they apply only to people in laboratories under the conditions Milgram arranged. And even if we assume a correspondence between laboratory behavior and more lifelike situations, no predictions can be made about *what* lifelike situations these might be. Neither can any serious claim be made that there is a causal relationship between the acceptance of legitimate authority and doing what you are told. In fact, Milgram himself shows us that there is not, since 35 percent of his subjects told the "authority figure" to bug off. Moreover, Milgram had no idea *why* some people did and some people did not tell him to bug off. For myself, I feel quite sure that if each of Milgram's subjects had been required to read Hannah Arendt's *Eichmann in Jerusalem* before showing up at the laboratory, Milgram's numbers would have been quite different.

But let us suppose that I am wrong about that, and let us further suppose that Milgram had found that 100 percent of his subjects did what they were told, with or without Hannah Arendt. And now let us suppose that I tell you a story of a group of people who in some real situation refused to comply with the orders of a legitimate authority. Would you say to me that this cannot be so, because Milgram's study proves otherwise? Or would you say that this overturns Milgram's work? I think you would say neither, because Milgram's experiment does not confirm or falsify any theory that might be said to postulate a law of human nature. His study, which incidentally I find both fascinating and terrifying, is not science. It is something else entirely.

Which leads me to say, at last, what sort of work I think Milgram was engaged in—and what sort of work all of us who study human behavior and situations are engaged in. I will start by making reference to a famous correspondence between Sigmund Freud and Albert Einstein. Freud once sent a copy of one of his books to Einstein, asking for his evaluation of it. Einstein replied that he thought the book exemplary but was not qualified to judge its scientific merit. To which Freud replied somewhat testily that if Einstein could say nothing of its scientific merit, he could not imagine how the book could be judged exemplary; it is science or it is nothing. Well, of course, Freud was wrong. His work *is* exemplary—indeed, monumental—but scarcely anyone believes today that Freud was doing science, any more than educated people believe that Marx was doing science, or Max Weber or Lewis Mumford or Bruno Bettelheim or Carl Jung or Margaret Mead or Arnold Toynbee. What these people were doing—and Stanley Milgram was doing—is weaving narratives about human behavior. Their work is a form of storytelling, not unlike conventional imaginative literature although different from it in several important ways.

I call the work these people do storytelling because this suggests that an author has given a unique interpretation to a set of human events, that he has supported his interpretation with examples in various forms, and that his interpretation cannot be proved or disproved but draws its appeal from the power of its language, the depth of its explanations, the relevance of its examples, and the credibility of its theme. And that all of this has an identifiable moral purpose. The words "true" and "false" do not apply here in the sense that they are used in mathematics or science. For there is nothing universally and irrevocably true or false about these interpretations. There are no critical tests to confirm or falsify them. There are no postulates in which they are embedded. They are bound by time, by situation, and above all by the cultural prejudices of the researcher. Quite like a piece of fiction.

A novelist—for example, D. H. Lawrence—tells a story about the sexual life of a woman, Lady Chatterley, and from it we may learn things about the secrets of some people, and wonder if Lady Chatterley's secrets are not more common than we had thought. Lawrence did not claim to be a scientist, but he looked carefully and deeply at the people he knew and concluded that there is more hypocrisy in heaven and earth than is dreamt of in some of our philosophies. Now, Alfred Kinsey was also interested in the sexual lives of women, and so he and his assistants interviewed thousands of them in an effort to find out what they believed their sexual conduct was like. Each woman told her story, although it was a story carefully structured by Kinsey's questions. Some of them told everything they were permitted to tell, some only a little, and some probably lied. But when all their tales were put together, a collective story emerged about a certain time and place. It was a story more abstract than D. H. Lawrence's, largely told in the language of statistics and, of course, without much psychological insight. But it was a story nonetheless. One might call it a tribal tale of one thousand and one nights, told by a thousand and one women, and its theme was not much different from Lawrence's—namely, that the sexual life of some women is a lot stranger and more active than some other stories, particularly Freud's, had led us to believe.

I do not say that there is no difference between Lawrence and Kinsey. Lawrence unfolds his story in a language structure called a narrative. Kinsey's language structure is called exposition. These forms are certainly different, although not so much as you might suppose. It has been remarked about the brothers Henry and William James that Henry was the novelist who wrote like a psychologist, and William the psychologist who wrote like a novelist. Certainly, in my meaning of the word "story," exposition is as capable of unfolding one as is narrative. Of course, Lawrence's story is controlled entirely by the limits of his own imagination, and he is not obliged to consult any social facts other than those he believed he knew. Lawrence's story is pure personal perception. And that is why we call it fiction. Kinsey's story comes from the mouths of others, and he is limited by what they said when he asked his questions. Kinsey's story, therefore, we may call a documentary. But like all stories, it is infused with moral prejudice and sociological theory. It is Kinsey who makes up the questions, and chooses who will be interviewed, the circumstances of the interview, and how the answers will be interpreted. All of this gives shape and point to his story. Indeed, we may assume that Kinsey, like Lawrence, knew from the outset what the theme of his story would be. Otherwise, he probably wouldn't have cared to tell it.

Both the novelist and the social researcher construct their stories by the use of archetypes and metaphors. Cervantes, for example, gave us the enduring archetype of the incurable dreamer and idealist in Don Quixote. The social historian Marx gave us the archetype of the ruthless and fat, though nameless, capitalist. Flaubert gave us the repressed bourgeois romantic in Emma Bovary. And Margaret Mead gave us the carefree, guiltless Samoan adolescent. Kafka gave us the alienated urbanite driven to self-loathing. And Max Weber gave us hardworking men driven by a mythology he called the Protestant Ethic. Dostoevsky gave us the egomaniac redeemed by love and religious fervor. And B. F. Skinner gives us the automaton redeemed by a benign technology.

I think it justifiable to say that in the nineteenth century, novelists provided us with most of the powerful metaphors and images of our culture. In the twentieth century, such metaphors and images have largely come from the pens of social historians and researchers. Think of John Dewey, William James, Erik Erikson, Alfred Kinsey, Thorstein Veblen, Margaret Mead, Lewis Mumford, B. F. Skinner, Carl Rogers, Marshall McLuhan, Noam Chomsky, even Stanley Milgram, and you must acknowledge that our ideas of what we are like and what kind of country we live in come from their stories to a far greater extent than from the stories of our most renowned novelists. I do not mean, incidentally, that I think the metaphors of social research are created in the same way as those of novels and plays. The writer of fiction creates metaphors by an elaborate and concrete detailing of the actions and feelings of particular human beings. Sociology is background; individual psychology is the focus. The researcher tends to do it the other way around. His focus is on a wider field, and the individual life is seen in silhouette, by inference and suggestion. Also, the novelists proceed by showing. The researchers, using abstract social facts, proceed by reason, by logic, by argument. That is why fiction is apt to be more entertaining. Whereas Oscar Wilde or Evelyn Waugh *shows* us the idle and conspicuously consuming rich,

Thorstein Veblen *argues* them into existence. In the character of Sammy Glick, Budd Schulberg *showed* us the narcissist whose origins Christopher Lasch has recently tried to *explain* through sociological analysis. So there are differences among storytellers, and most of the time our novelists are more pleasurable to read. But the stories told by our social researchers are at least as compelling and, in our own times, apparently more credible.

What I am driving at is this: Once we rid ourselves of the false notion that we are scientists, and accept the idea that we are among our culture's most important tellers of psychological and social tales, the answers to the two questions I began with are obvious. As to what are legitimate forms of research into human communication, we may answer by permitting ourselves the greatest possible latitude. Historical speculation, philosophical argument, literary criticism, case histories, biography, semantic and semiotic analysis, ethnography—all these and more ought to be admissible as ways of telling our stories, and the less concern about method, the better. One becomes fastidious about method only when one has no story to tell. The best people in our field have, with few exceptions, been almost indifferent to the question of method. Who can characterize Harold Innis's method? Or Susanne Langer's? Or Eric Havelock's? Or McLuhan's? Or Mumford's? Or Jacques Ellul's? They used whatever social or historical theories and facts seemed relevant; they put forward their arguments by using the instruments of reason, logic, intuition, conjecture. Even Erving Goffman, who seems more technical than most, hasn't much of a method; what he has is a metaphor: that life is a stage and we are all players on it. Of course, we can also count things, if we wish, and do correlational studies. But if we do, we ought to make it clear what social theory is serving as the frame for our story. George Gerbner does such studies, but only because he wants to tell a story of a people slowly, perhaps inexorably, being overcome by feelings of powerlessness. Stanley Milgram did such studies because he wanted to demonstrate that a commonplace of human experience—what we know about ourselves—can be more terrifying than what we don't know. Alfred Kinsey did such studies because he believed that official morality is, and probably always has been, rubbish.

And so, the answer to the first question is that by resisting the attractions of pseudo-science, and embracing the role of creators and narrators of social myth, media ecologists can enrich our field of study immeasurably. Of course, this cannot be done without risk. It means that most of us will generate piles of junk—unconvincing stories without credible documentation, sound logic, or persuasive argument. After all, how many Lewis Mumfords or Walter Ongs or Lynn Whites or Jacques Elluls are there? But then, how many Franz Kafkas, D. H. Lawrences, or James Joyces are there? It is a risk that must be borne. The alternative is to remain a shriveled pseudo-science, useless for everything except the assembly-line production of Ph.D.s.

As for my second question—What is the purpose of such research?—the answer is *not*, obviously, to contribute to our field, but to contribute to human understanding and decency. For the most part, novelists do not write to enrich the field of novel-writing. The good ones write because they are angry or curious or cynical or enchanted. *The Scarlet Letter* was not written by a man who wanted to improve the art of the novel, but by a man who wanted to improve the art of living together. Similarly, *The Myth of the Machine, Understanding Media, The Technological Society, Computer Power and Human Reason, Stigma, Anger, Public Opinion*, and, if you will pardon an attempt to gilt myself by association, *Amusing Ourselves to Death*—all these books were written by men and women who were concerned not to improve scholarship but to improve social life. Thus, the purpose of doing this kind of work is essentially didactic and moralistic. These men and women tell their stories for the same reason the Buddha, Confucius, Hillel, and Jesus told their stories. To put it plainly, the so-called social sciences are subdivisions of moral theology. It is true, of course, that social researchers rarely base their claims to knowledge on the indisputability of sacred texts, and even less so on revelation. But you must not be dazzled or deluded by differences in method between preachers and scholars. Without meaning to be blasphemous, I would say that Jesus was as keen a sociologist as Veblen. Indeed, Jesus' remark about rich men, camels, and the eye of a needle is as good a summary of Veblen's *Theory of the Leisure Class* as it is possible to make. As social researchers, Jesus and Veblen differed in that Veblen was more garrulous.

Like moral theology, social research never discovers anything. It only rediscovers what people once were told and need to be told again. If, indeed, the price of civilization is repressed sexuality, it was not Sigmund Freud who discovered it. If the consciousness of people is formed by their material circumstances, it was not Marx who discovered it. If the medium is the message, it was not McLuhan who discovered it.

The purpose of social research is to rediscover the truths of social life; to comment on and criticize the moral behavior of people; and finally, to put forward metaphors, images, and ideas that can help people live with some measure of understanding and dignity. Specifically, the purpose of media ecology is to tell stories about the consequences of technology; to tell how media environments create contexts that may change the way we think or organize our social life, or make us better or worse, or smarter or dumber, or freer or more enslaved. I feel sure the reader will pardon a touch of bias when I say that the stories media ecologists have to tell are rather more important than those of other academic storytellers—because the power of communication technology to give shape to people's lives is not a matter that comes easily to the forefront of people's consciousness, though we live in an age when our lives—whether we like it or not—have been submitted to the demanding sovereignty of new media. And so we are obliged, in the interest of a humane survival, to tell tales about what sort of paradise may be gained, and what sort lost. We will not have been the first to tell such tales. But unless our stories ring true, we may be the last.

Defending Against the Indefensible

This essay originated as a lecture I gave in The Hague, Holland, to an audience of people who teach in English-language independent schools throughout Europe. I should stress that they were not primarily teachers of English, whom I have for the most part stopped addressing, since I came to the conclusion several years ago that they are the educators least likely to depart in any significant way from their pedagogical traditions. I do not know why this is so, but it is a serious deficiency, since English teachers are better positioned than any others to cultivate intelligence.

I am sure many of you will recognize that my title derives from a phrase in George Orwell's famous essay "Politics and the English Language." In that essay, Orwell speaks of the dangerously degraded condition of modern political thought, and proceeds to characterize its language as mainly committed to "defending the indefensible."

In the thirty-five years or so since Orwell wrote his essay, it has become even more obvious that the principal purpose of most political language is to justify or, if possible, to make glorious the malignant ambitions of nation states. Perhaps it has always been so—at least since the seventeenth century—and I don't suppose many of us expect it to be different in the future. With the exception of the much misunderstood Machiavelli, no one ever said politics is a pretty profession, and if Orwell thought it could be otherwise, he was an optimist.

I, too, am an optimist. But not because I look for any improvement in the purposes of political discourse. I am an optimist because I think it might just be possible for people to learn how to recognize empty, false, self-serving, or inhumane language, and therefore to protect themselves from at least some of its spiritually debasing consequences. My optimism places me in the camp of H. G. Wells, who said that civilization is in a race between education and disaster, and that although education is far behind, it is not yet out of the running. In other words, while I do not think we can count on any relaxation in the defense of the indefensible, I believe we may mount a practical counteroffensive by better preparing the minds of those for whom such language is intended.

Thus our attention inevitably turns to the subject of schools and to the possibility of their actually doing something that would help our youth acquire the semantic sophistication that we associate with minds unburdened by prejudice and provinciality. Of course, I am well aware that in most of the world, school is the last place you would expect such an education to be seriously conducted; in most places, school is conceived of as a form of indoctrination, the continuation of politics by gentle means.

The idea that schooling should make the young compliant and easily accessible to the prejudices of their society is an old and venerable tradition. This function of education was clearly advocated by our two earliest and greatest curriculum specialists, Confucius and Plato. Their writings created the tradition that requires educators to condition the young to believe what they are told, in the way they are told it.

But the matter does not rest there. We are fortunate to have available an alternative tradition that gives us the authority to educate our students to *disbelieve* or at least to be skeptical of the prejudices of their elders. We can locate the origins of this tradition in some fragments from Cicero, who remarked that the purpose of education is to free the student from the tyranny of the present. We find elaborations of this point of view in Descartes, Bacon, Vico, Goethe, and Jefferson. And we find its modern resonances in John Dewey, Freud, and Bertrand Russell.

It is in the spirit of this tradition—that is, education as a defense *against* culture—that I wish to speak. I will not address the important issue of how such an education in disbelief can be made palatable to those who pay for our schools. I know next to nothing about that, and what I know seems to be wrong. Rather, my remarks are aimed at those who would be interested to know how one might proceed if one had the authority and the desire to do so.

The method I have chosen for this purpose is to provide you with seven concepts, all of which have to do with language. I will not presume to call these concepts the Seven Pillars of Wisdom, but I believe that, if taken seriously, they have the potential to clear away some of the obtuseness that makes minds vulnerable to indefensible discourse. Before setting them out, I must stress that the education I speak of is *not* confined to helping students immunize themselves against the *politically* indefensible. Such an education would be in itself indefensible, and, fortunately, there is no need for it. We can assume that if we find a way to promote critical intelligence through language education, such intelligence can defend itself against almost anything that is indefensible—from Newspeak to commercial huckstering to bureaucratese

to that most debilitating of all forms of nonsense that afflict
the young, school textbooks. The assumption that critical
intelligence has wide applicability is, I believe, what the medieval Schoolmen had in mind in creating the Trivium, which
in their version consisted of grammar, logic, and rhetoric.
These arts of language were assumed to be what may be called
"meta-subjects," subjects about subjects. Their rules, guidelines, principles, and insights were thought to be useful in
thinking about *anything*. Our ancestors understood well
something we seem to have forgotten, namely, that all subjects are forms of discourse—indeed, forms of literature—
and therefore that almost all education is language education.
Knowledge of a subject mostly means knowledge of the language of that subject. Biology, after all, is not plants and
animals; it is language about plants and animals. History is
not events that once occurred; it is language describing and
interpreting events. And astronomy is not planets and stars
but a special way of talking about planets and stars.

And so a student must know the language of a subject,
but that is only the beginning. For it is not sufficient to know
the definition of a noun, or a gene, or a molecule. One must
also know what a definition is. It is not sufficient to know
the right answers. One must also know the questions that
produced them. Indeed, one must know what a question is,
for not every sentence that ends with a rising intonation or
begins with an interrogative is necessarily a question. There
are sentences that look like questions but cannot generate
any meaningful answers, and if they linger in our minds, they
become obstructions to clear thinking. One must also know
what a metaphor is and what is the relationship between
words and the things they describe. In short, one must have
some knowledge of a meta-language—a language about language. Without such knowledge, a student can be as easily
tyrannized by a subject as by a politician. That is to say, the

enemy here is not, in the end, indefensible discourse but our ignorance of how to proceed against it.

Now, what I want to recommend to you is not so systematic or profound as the Trivium. I do not even propose a new subject—only seven ideas or insights or principles (call them what you will) that are essential to the workings of the critical intelligence and that are in the jurisdiction of every teacher at every level of school.

My first principle is about the process of definition. Most people are overcome by a sort of intellectual paralysis when confronted by a definition, whether offered by a politician or by a teacher. They fail to grasp that a definition is not a manifestation of nature but merely and always an instrument for helping us to achieve our purposes. I. A. Richards once remarked, "We want to do something, and a definition is a means of doing it. If we want certain results, then we must use certain definitions. But no definition has any authority apart from a purpose, or any authority to bar us from other purposes." This is one of the most liberating statements I know. But I have, myself, never heard a student ask of a teacher, "Whose definition is that and what purposes are served by it?" It is more than likely that a teacher would be puzzled by such a question, for most of us have been as tyrannized by definitions as have our students. But I do know of one instance where a student refused to accept a definition provided by an entire school. The student applied to Columbia University for admission and was rejected. In response, he sent the following letter to the admissions officer:

Dear Sir:
I am in receipt of your rejection of my application. As much as I would like to accommodate you, I find I cannot. I have already received four rejections from other colleges, which is, in fact, my limit. Your re-

jection puts me over this limit. Therefore, I must reject
your rejection, and as much as this might inconve-
nience you, I expect to appear for classes on September 18. . . .

Columbia would have been well advised to reconsider this
student's application, not because it doesn't have a right to
define for its own purposes what it means by an adequate
student, but because here is a student who understands what
some of Columbia's professors probably do not—that there
is a measure of arbitrariness in every definition and that in
any case an intelligent person is not required to accept another's definition, even if he can't do much about it.

What students need to be taught, then, is that definitions
are not given to us by God; that we may depart from them
without risking our immortal souls; that the authority of a
definition rests entirely on its usefulness, not on its correctness
(whatever that means); and that it is a form of stupidity to
accept without reflection someone else's definition of a word,
a problem, or a situation. All of this applies as much to a
definition of a verb or a molecule as it does to a definition
of art, God, freedom, or democracy. I can think of no better
method of helping students to defend themselves than to provide them with alternative definitions for every important
concept and term they must deal with in school. It is essential
that they understand that definitions are hypotheses and that
embedded in each is a particular philosophical or political or
epistemological point of view. It is certainly true that he who
holds the power to define is our master, but it is also true
that he who holds in mind an alternative definition can never
quite be his slave.

My second concept is best introduced by a story attributed to the American psychologist Gordon Allport. He tells
of two priests who were engaged in a dispute on whether or

not it is permissible to pray and smoke at the same time. One believed that it is, the other that it is not, and so each decided to write to the Pope for a definitive answer. After doing so, they met again to share their results and were astonished to discover that the Pope had agreed with both of them. "How did you pose the question?" the first asked. The other replied, "I asked if it is permissible to smoke while praying. His Holiness said that it is not, since praying is a very serious business. And how did you phrase the question?" The first replied, "I asked if it is permissible to pray while smoking, and His Holiness said that it is, since it is always appropriate to pray."

The point of this story, of course, is that the form in which we ask our questions will determine the answers we get. To put it more broadly: all the knowledge we ever have is a result of questions. Indeed, it is a commonplace among scientists that they do not see nature as it is, but only through the questions they put to it. I should go further: we do not see *anything* as it is except through the questions we put to it. And there is a larger point even than this: since questions are the most important intellectual tool we have, is it not incredible that the art and science of question-asking is not systematically taught? I would suggest that we correct this deficiency and not only put question-asking on our teaching agenda but place it near the top of the list. After all, in a profound sense, it is meaningless to have answers if we do not know the questions that produced them—whether in biology, grammar, politics, or history. To have an answer without knowing the question, without understanding that you might have been given a different answer if the question had been posed differently, may be more than meaningless; it may be exceedingly dangerous. There are many Americans who carry in their heads such answers as "America should proceed at once with our Star Wars project," or, "We should send

Marines to Nicaragua." But if they do not know the questions to which these are the answers, their opinions are quite literally thoughtless. And so I suggest two things. First, we should teach our students something about question-asking in general. For example, that a vaguely formed question produces a vaguely formed answer; that every question has a point of view embedded in it; that for any question that is posed, there is almost always an alternative question that will generate an alternative answer; that every action we take is an answer to a question, even if we are not aware of it; that ineffective actions may be the result of badly formed questions; and most of all, that a question is language, and therefore susceptible to all the errors to which an unsophisticated understanding of language can lead. As Francis Bacon put it more than 350 years ago: "There arises from a bad and unapt formation of words a wonderful obstruction to the mind." This is as good a definition of stupidity as I know: a bad and unapt formation of words. Let us, then, go "back to Bacon," and study the art of question-asking. But we must also focus on the specific details of asking questions in different subjects. What, for example, are the sorts of questions that obstruct the mind, or free it, in the study of history? How are these questions different from those one might ask of a mathematical proof, or a literary work, or a biological theory? The principles and rules of asking questions obviously differ as we move from one system of knowledge to another, and this ought not to be ignored.

Which leads me to my third principle: namely, that the most difficult words in any form of discourse are rarely the polysyllabic ones that are hard to spell and which send students to their dictionaries. The troublesome words are those whose meanings appear to be simple, like "true," "false," "fact," "law," "good," and "bad." A word like "participle" or "mutation" or "centrifugal," or, for that matter, "apartheid" or "proletariat," rarely raises serious problems in understanding. The range of situations in which such a word might appear is limited and does not tangle us in ambiguity. But a word like "law" is used in almost every universe of discourse, and with different meanings in each. "The law of supply and demand" is a different "law" from "Grimm's Law" in linguistics or "Newton's Law" in physics or "the law of the survival of the fittest" in biology. What is a "true" statement in mathematics is different from a "true" statement in economics, and when we speak of the "truth" of a literary work, we mean something else again. Moreover, when President Reagan says it is "right" to place cruise missiles in Europe, he does not appeal to the same authority or even logic as when he says it is "right" to reduce the national deficit. And when Karl Marx said it was "right" for the working class to overthrow the bourgeoisie, he meant something different altogether, as does a teacher who proclaims it is "right" to say "he doesn't" instead of "he don't."

If we insist on giving our students vocabulary tests, then for God's sake let us find out if they know something about the truly difficult words in the language. I think it would be entirely practical to design a curriculum based on an inquiry into, let us say, fifty hard words, beginning with "good" and "bad" and ending with "true" and "false." Show me a student who knows something about what these words imply, what sources of authority they appeal to, and in what circumstances they are used, and I will show you a student who is an epistemologist—which is to say, a student who knows what textbooks try to conceal. And a student who knows what textbooks try to conceal will know what advertisers try to conceal, and politicians and preachers, as well.

Fourth, I think it would also be practical to design a curriculum based on an inquiry into the use of metaphor. Unless I am sorely mistaken, metaphor is at present rarely approached in school except by English teachers during lessons in poetry. This strikes me as absurd, since I do not see how it is possible for a subject to be understood in the absence of any insight into the metaphors on which it is constructed. All subjects are based on powerful metaphors that direct and organize the way we will do our thinking. In history, economics, physics, biology, and linguistics, metaphors, like questions, are organs of perception. Through our metaphors, we see the world as one thing or another. Is light a wave or a particle? An astrophysicist I know tells me that she and her colleagues don't know, and so at the moment they settle for the word "wavicle." Are molecules like billiard balls or force fields? Is language like a tree (some say it has roots) or a river (some say it has tributaries) or a building (some say it has foundations)? Is history unfolding according to some instructions of nature or according to a divine plan? Are our genes like information codes? Is a literary work like an architect's blueprint or is it a mystery the reader must solve? Questions like these preoccupy scholars in every field because they are what is basic to the field itself. Nowhere is this more so than in education. Rousseau begins his great treatise on education, *Emile,* with the following words: "Plants are improved by cultivation, and men by education." And his entire philosophy is made to rest upon this comparison of plants and children.

There is no test, textbook, syllabus, or lesson plan that any of us creates that does not reflect our preference for some metaphor of the mind, or of knowledge, or of the process of learning. Do you believe a student's mind to be a muscle that must be exercised? Or a garden that must be cultivated? Or a dark cavern that must be illuminated? Or an empty vessel that must be filled to overflowing? Whichever you favor, your metaphor will control—often without your being aware of it—how you will proceed as a teacher. This is as true of politicians as it is of academics. No political practitioner has ever spoken three consecutive sentences without invoking some metaphorical authority for his actions. And this is especially true of powerful political theorists. Rousseau begins *The Social Contract* with a powerful metaphor that Marx was to use later, and many times: "Man is born free but is everywhere in chains." Marx himself begins *The Communist Manifesto* with an ominous and ghostly metaphor—the famous "A specter haunts Europe . . ." Abraham Lincoln, in his celebrated Gettysburg Address, compares America's forefathers to God when he says they "brought forth a new nation," just as God brought forth the heavens and the earth. And Adolf Hitler concludes *Mein Kampf* with this: "A state which in this age of racial poisoning dedicates itself to the care of its best racial elements must someday become the lord of the earth." All forms of discourse are metaphor-laden, and unless our students are aware of how metaphors shape arguments, organize perceptions, and control feelings, their understanding is severely limited.

Which gets me to my fifth concept, what is called reification. Reification means confusing words with things. It is a thinking error with multiple manifestations, some merely amusing, others extremely dangerous. This past summer in the sweltering New York heat, a student of mine looked at a thermometer in our classroom. "It's ninety-six degrees," he said. "No wonder it's so hot!" He had it the wrong way around, of course, as many people do who have never learned or cannot remember these three simple notions: that there are things in the world and then there are our names for them; that there is no such thing as a real name; and that a name may or may not suggest the nature of the thing named—as, for example, when the United States government called its South Pacific hydrogen-bomb experiments Operation Sunshine. What I am trying to say here is what Shakespeare said more eloquently in his line "A rose by any other name would smell as sweet." But Shakespeare was only half right, in that for many people a rose would *not* smell as sweet if it were called a "stinkweed." And because this is so, because people confuse names with things, advertising is among the most consistently successful enterprises in the world today. Advertisers know that no matter how excellent an automobile may be, it will not sell if it is called the "Lumbering Elephant." More important, they know that no matter how rotten a car may be, you *can* sell it if it is called a "Vista Cruiser" or a "Phoenix" or a "Grand Prix." Politicians know this as well, and, sad to say, so do scholars, who far too often obscure the emptiness of what they are talking and writing about by affixing alluring names to what is not there. I suggest, therefore, that reification be given a prominent place in our studies, so that our students will know how it both works and works them over.

Sixth, some attention must be given to the style and tone of language. Each universe of discourse has its own special way of addressing its subject matter and its audience. Each subject in a curriculum is a special manner of speaking and writing, with its own rhetoric of knowledge, a characteristic way in which arguments, proofs, speculations, experiments, polemics, even humor, are expressed. Speaking and writing are, after all, performing arts, and each subject requires a somewhat different kind of performance. Historians, for example, do not speak or write history in the same way biologists speak or write biology. The differences have to do with the degree of precision their generalizations permit, the types of facts they marshal, the traditions of their subject, and the nature of their training. It is worth remembering that many scholars have exerted influence as much through their manner as their matter—one thinks of Veblen in sociology, Freud in psychology, Galbraith in economics. The point is that knowledge is a form of literature, and the various styles of knowledge ought to be studied and discussed, all the more because the language found in typical school textbooks tends to obscure this. Textbook language, which is apt to be the same from subject to subject, creates the false impression that systematic knowledge is always expressed in a dull, uninspired monotone. I have read recipes on the back of cereal boxes that were written with more style and conviction than textbook descriptions of the causes of the American Revolution. Of the language of grammar books I will not even speak, for, to borrow from Shakespeare, it is unfit for a Christian ear to endure. But the problem is not insurmountable. Teachers who are willing to take the time can find materials that convey ideas in a form characteristic of their discipline. And while they are at it, they can help their students to see that what we call a prayer, a political speech, and an advertisement differ from each other not only in their content but in their style and tone; one might say *mostly* in their style and tone and manner of address.

Which brings me to the seventh and final concept—what I shall call the principle of the non-neutrality of media. I mean by this what Marshall McLuhan meant to suggest when he said, "The medium is the message": that the form in which information is coded has, itself, an inescapable bias. In a certain sense, this is an entirely familiar idea. We recognize, for example, that the world is somewhat different when we speak about it in English and when we speak about it in German. We might even say that the grammar of a language is an organ of perception and accounts for the variances in world view that we find among different peoples. But we have been slow to acknowledge that every extension of speech—from painting to hieroglyphics to the alphabet to the printing press to television—also generates unique ways of apprehending the world, amplifying or obscuring different features of reality.

Each medium, like language itself, classifies the world for us, sequences it, frames it, enlarges it, reduces it, argues a case for what the world is like. In the United States, for example, it is no longer possible for a fat person to be elected to high political office—not because our Constitution forbids it but because television forbids it, since television exalts the attractive visual image and has little patience with or love for the subtle or logical word.

Our students must understand two essential points about all this. Just as language itself creates culture in its own image, each new medium of communication re-creates or modifies culture in *its* image; and it is extreme naïveté to believe that a medium of communication or, indeed, any technology is merely a tool, a way of doing. Each is also a way of *seeing*. To a man with a hammer, everything looks like a nail. To a man with a pencil, everything looks like a sentence; to a man with a television camera, everything looks like a picture; and to a man with a computer, the whole world looks like data. To put it another way, and to paraphrase the philosopher Wittgenstein, a medium of communication may be a vehicle of thought but we must not forget that it is also the driver. A consideration of how the printing press or the telegraph or television or the computer does its driving and where it takes us must be included in our students' education or else they will be disarmed and extremely vulnerable.

There is one more principle about language that is probably occurring to many of you right about now: namely, that one ought not to put up with any lecturer who takes more of your time than he has been allotted. And so I will conclude with three points. First, I trust you understand that the suggestions I have made are not directed exclusively or even primarily at language teachers, English or otherwise. This is a task for everyone. Second, I want to reiterate that to provide our students with a defense against the indefensible, it is neither necessary nor desirable to focus exclusively on political language. Whenever this is attempted, it is apt to be shallow and limited. The best defense is one with a wider reach, which has implications for all language transactions. And finally, I do not claim that my proposals will solve all our problems, or even provide full protection from indefensible discourse. They are only a reasonable beginning, and there is much more to be done. But we have to start somewhere and, as Ray Bradbury once wrote, somewhere lies between the right ear and the left.

The Naming
of Missiles

*I offer this piece (and three similar ones further on) with
the knowledge that satire or parody is increasingly difficult
to write in our time. The eleven o'clock television news and
the front pages of our newspapers compete with our imagination's attempts to create the bizarre. Reality is now not
only stranger than fiction but a stranger to common sense.*

In consideration of our country's unlimited devotion to
democratic principles, it is altogether proper that on January 10 of next year, officials at Cape Canaveral will con-
vene a two-week public conference on the naming of missiles.

To be known officially as the Conference on Democratic
Missile Nomenclature, this unprecedented convention will
provide groups from all over the country with an opportunity
to exert an influence in choosing the names of our nation's
missiles.

The official announcement of the conference stressed the
following: "The important point to remember is that every
missile we make is *everybody's* missile, paid for by *everybody's* money, and propelled by *everybody's* faith in its peace-
ful purpose. Therefore, all citizens should have some voice

in deciding what our missiles should be named. That is the essence of democracy, as we here at the Cape understand it."

The guiding genius behind the conference (he calls himself, with characteristic grace, "the *gliding* genius") is Major General Francis ("Rosey") Logan, a subtle but gregarious Texan who is chief of Cape Canaveral's public-relations division. As slow-speaking as he is quick-witted, General Logan despises all forms of totalitarianism with an intensity unusual even for Cape Canaveral personnel. "The amazing thing about most people," he likes to observe, "is that they think missiles are born with names, the way kids are. Nothing could be further from the truth. Actually, no one knows what a missile's name is until someone consciously chooses it."

Until now, the American public has had almost nothing to do with that choice. In point of fact, for the past ten years, one man—and only one—has been in charge of naming our missiles. He was the late Michael Protopopolus, a grim, iron-willed, former college professor with an unbridled passion for all things Greek, classical, and classically Greek. As a consequence, along with their awesome payload, most of our important missiles carry such awesome names as Saturn, Atlas, Jupiter, Nike, and Zeus.

Protopopolus, who was killed in an accident at the Cape last October, not only was responsible for proposing names for all new missiles but also had the power to approve or reject names proposed by other people. Apparently, he would on occasion permit some non-Hellenic name (for example, Challenger) to be used, but only when he felt that the missile itself was defective and that its manufacture would quite likely be abandoned.

Upon Protopopolus's death, his position was filled by Dr. Marvin S. Feldstein, a nuclear physicist (with a passion for semantics) from the University of Chicago. It became apparent at once that Feldstein's appointment was a mistake. His first four proposals—the Talmud, the Diaspora, the Exodus, and the Mishna—were an embarrassment to all those at the Cape, particularly to those German physicists and engineers who are, for all their advancing years, still mainly responsible for designing the missiles. Fortunately, Feldstein was accused of being a latent homosexual, and, as a consequence, summarily relieved of his duties and sent packing back to Chicago.

"All of that unpleasantness is behind us now," says Logan. "With the exception of the Mishna, none of the Jewish missiles turned out to be very good and we have ceased producing them. The Mishna, ironically, is now shipped exclusively to Arab countries, where, of course, it can freely be renamed. In any case," he continues, "we hope that the conference will be an annual affair and thus provide us with enough names for each year's supply of missiles."

The organization of the conference will be simple. Any group of citizens wishing to propose a name or names may apply *before* April 1 to:

The Conference on Democratic Missile Nomenclature
c/o Maj. Gen. Francis Logan
Public Relations Division
Cape Canaveral, FLA.

One spokesman for each group will be allowed to address the entire conference for fifteen minutes. During his allotted time, he must state what group he represents, what name or names he is proposing, and his reasons for believing that such a name does credit to this country. The last two days of the conference will be spent in voting on the various proposals, with each group being permitted one vote.

According to General Logan, the response to the conference has already been gratifying. Within twelve hours of the announcement's being made, no fewer than sixteen groups had applied for speaking time, among them the Longshoremen's Union, the Federation of Eastern Seaboard Presbyterian Ministers, the Tulsa University Chapter of Hillel, and the Baton Rouge Division of the White Citizens' Council.

Perhaps the most interesting and forthright group to apply so far is the Physicists and Engineers of Teutonic Institutes of Science. The group's spokesman, Dr. Erik Schreiber, is a brilliant but eccentric eighty-two-year-old rocket-fuel specialist who since 1950 has for some curious reason defected two times to the East and two times back to the West.

Among the most respected of all the rocket engineers at the Cape, he says, in perfect English: "Moral, social, and ethical questions aside, our group feels entitled to propose a name or two, since you might say that we make the things you Americans wish to name." With a quick and slightly intimidating smile, he adds, in perfect Russian: "After all, you might say that if our group defected to the East, there would be no missile program at the Cape."

Indeed there would not, and General Logan, cognizant of this fact, is an open partisan of Schreiber's cause. He drawls, "They plan to suggest only one name—the Deutschland Über Alles—and although I think it is a bit long, you cannot say it is unreasonable. In any case, I think we owe it to these courageous and imaginative men to give their suggestion the most careful consideration."

Since, in the eyes of many, the principal reason for our having a missile program at all is the defense and perpetuation of Christianity, even more careful consideration will doubtless be given to the suggestions made by various Christian organizations. The most articulate and colorful of these is the Friends of Cardinal O'Connor, a militant group of Catholic Army officers which feels that to date our "missile program, namewise, has been atheistic." To correct this condition, the group will suggest three names—the Apostle, the Inquisition, and the Encyclical.

Their plan calls for the Encyclical to be used exclusively as the name of any missile which carries a hydrogen-bomb warhead. Their reasoning is cogently expressed by their spokesman, Colonel Harvey Washburn, a former Benedictine monk who sometimes serves as military adviser to Cardinal O'Connor. He says, "When an Encyclical is launched, we'll know that our atheistic enemies will get the message."

To which General Logan, a Catholic himself, adds, "Amen."

Already apparent, the major obstacle to the success of the conference will be crank groups proposing absurd or vicious names. For example, one group calling itself the University of Chicago Jewish Professors Executive Council has suggested a name, the Matzoh Fry, for all ICBMs. General Logan believes that, in fact, there is no such group and that the suggestion comes from Dr. Marvin Feldstein, the latent homosexual, who may still harbor resentment against those who dismissed him from the Cape.

Other groups of fictitious origin have suggested such names as the Disfigurer, the Holocaust, and the Incinerator. Needless to say, flippancy of this nature would drive most men into a frenzy, but General Logan remains almost stoic. He comments quietly, "It is simply beyond me to comprehend how anyone can even attempt levity about such things."

General Logan steadfastly refuses to predict the results of the conference. "There are two things of which I am sure," he concludes. "The first is that at long last our country's missiles will be properly and democratically named. The second is that the conference will unanimously pass my resolution to name this year's largest missile the Great Communicator."

To which we can all add a heartfelt "Amen."

My German Question

In the summer of 1985, I was offered an astonishing opportunity by the famous German magazine Stern. *I was asked to take a leisurely tour of Germany (all expenses paid), keep my eyes and ears open, and then write an essay on my impressions. The same opportunity was offered to ten or so other writers, including Anthony Burgess and Alberto Moravia. We did not meet, made our tours at different times, and, of course, wrote about entirely different aspects of German culture. My essay appeared in* Stern *in October 1985. This is the first appearance of the essay in its original English.*

The great German physicist Werner Heisenberg remarked that nature does not reveal itself as it is but only through the questions we put to it. If this is true of our encounters with nature, surely it is even more true of our encounters with a nation. And truer still when the person asking questions of the German nation is a foreigner who, as a child, trembled at the mere sound of the German language, who was nurtured to feel about Germany as Luther did of the papacy: that it is an abomination in the sight of the Lord.

But not an unqualified abomination. As hard as it tried,

my education could not conceal that Germany had produced the world's most beautiful music, its most rigorous science, some of its deepest philosophy, and its tenderest and most penetrating literature. Thus, even as the Nazis were organizing their answer to the Jewish Question, there vaguely formed in my child-mind what I came to call the Question of German Schizophrenia. On the one hand, about half of the heritage of Western humanism and learning is of German origin. On the other, there is an ancient, mystical German impulse to barbarism that has cost world civilization dearly and that found its most recent and hideous expression in Auschwitz, the madmen who invented it, and the people who nourished them. Is this not a form of cultural schizophrenia? Could this be what the great Goethe meant when he said, "I have often felt a bitter sorrow at the thought of the German people, which are so estimable in the individual and so wretched in the generality"? Has anyone remarked on the fact that the three men who gave Germany its national voice in language and religion (Luther), in music (Wagner), and in philosophy (Nietzsche) were close to being clinically schizophrenic? Is there any other culture with so many geniuses whose humane creativity was clouded over by weird and dark impulses? (I include here Frederick the Great, Hegel, Schopenhauer, and Marx, among others.) Is it merely an accident of history that Germany is now split into two halves, or is this a precise and inevitable metaphor of German consciousness?

Of course, when I was a child, I did not have the words to put my German Question clearly. But now it is different. I came to Germany prepared. My hope was to make Germany reveal itself (or to make it reveal *myself*) by such questions as the following: Is German cultural schizophrenia my personal delusion? If not, is it a feature of the German character? If it is, how does it show itself in everyday life? Does it make

Germans an uncommonly dangerous people? Or uncommonly creative? Or both?

Well, it is easy enough to ask such questions. But to know where and how to find the answers is another matter. As it turned out (and so often does when one undertakes a journey of discovery), I did not exactly find the answers to the questions I began with but, instead, found an answer of extreme importance to a question absent from my agenda.

My odyssey began in Munich, took me to Frankfurt, and, with several stops in between, ended in Hamburg. In Munich, I witnessed an extraordinary moment which, I thought, clearly exemplified the kind of character discontinuity I was looking for. I had the good fortune to participate in a conference of educators and businessmen who were concerned with the impact of technology on German culture. Before the speeches began, the participants exchanged amiable greetings in the hallway. There were animated conversations, much good humor, stimulating queries; in short, one saw intelligent people expressing their enthusiasm for their subject and for one another. And then they assembled for the speeches, of which there were eight, each a half-hour long. As the participants crossed the threshold of the auditorium where the speeches were to be given, their demeanor was radically transformed. They seemed to leave their personalities in the hallway as one might leave one's coat and hat. Of course, to some extent this is inevitable whenever individuals become a group. But something was different here. The faces of the audience became impassive and their bodies rigid, and that is the condition in which they remained as the speakers talked on. No time was allotted for questions, and one felt that, in any case, none would be asked. No one left the auditorium for any reason. Is it possible, I wondered, that Germans can exercise such control over their bladders that no one needs to use the bathroom in four hours? Or can exercise such control over their patience that boredom does not drive them out of the room? Does no one want a cigarette or need to make a telephone call? Does no one feel it necessary to express displeasure or disagreement with a scowl or a sneer? To an American, the scene was astonishing, all the more so because no one else seemed aware of anything unusual. Is this the legendary German obedience and reverence for formality of which one has always heard so much? Had I come face to face with the essence of German character, and so soon?

The answer, as it turned out, was "No." I did not realize it then, but that afternoon in an auditorium in Munich was the last time the question of German character seemed relevant. As I moved through Germany talking to everyone who would talk to me, including TMOS (The Man On the Street), the question of "character" began to recede. At the end, it had disappeared altogether, to be replaced by a question about the German "situation." Gradually, I began to take my "schizophrenia" metaphor more seriously, for in clinical terms a split personality is not a matter of a character deficiency but a response to one's inability to resolve an intolerably paradoxical situation. I soon realized that if I were to find evidence of cultural schizophrenia, I would have to find it in situation, not character.

The day following the Munich conference, I began to see that more clearly. I visited (if that is the word) Dachau, where an aunt and uncle of mine had perished. While there, I was struck by the thought that, in itself, the Dachau Memorial is an example of an intolerable paradox. It tries to speak of the unspeakable, and what results is a sickly inhuman wail. I heard a guide tell a group of foreign high-school students that Germans knew nothing of what had happened in Dachau. He insisted that his parents had learned of the camp from a *Manchester Guardian* newspaper clipping sent to them after the war by relatives in England. I was stunned by his absurd delusion of innocence. But what did I expect him to say? That everyone knew? That Germany was, in fact, populated by a legion of lunatics? I wondered what I might say were I in his place. I wondered, too, what sort of memorial I would have designed had I been a "good" German and had been asked to do so. Somehow, I felt it would not be this. The place is good-looking, neat, clean, and far from terrifying. A quiet stream runs through part of it. The barracks are gone. The death buildings are approached through a cool and verdant arbor. This is all hideously wrong, I thought. But why? What did I expect? Bones in the courtyard? Electronically produced screams from well-placed stereo speakers? It is hard to say, and the question still haunts me. I left Dachau feeling only that here is history hiding from itself. It is a situation that has no solution.

Later that day, I had lunch with three young Germans, one of whom was a woman in her late twenties. I mentioned that I had been to Dachau, which prompted the young woman to embark on a sincere lament over man's inhumanity to man. She spoke of the oppression of the Irish by the English, and the ways in which American colonists conquered the Indians. She also cited the Turkish massacre of the Armenians, and when it became clear that her course was fixed on taking me all the way back to Genghis Khan, I interrupted. I told her that my sensitivity to man's inhumanity to man needed no improvement. But she seemed intent on finishing her discourse, which she did ten minutes later by remarking that starvation and despair will always produce horrors. I answered: "What happened in Dachau requires a different explanation from the other examples you give." There was a pause, after which she began to cry; softly at first, then more energetically. I filled the room with apologies. "This was not the time or place for such a challenge," I said. "Besides, you were born in 1959. What does Dachau have to do with you?" "You underestimate us," she replied. "It has everything to do with us. And you were right to say what you did. We Germans do not look our past in the eye. It will make us crazy someday."

Two days later, I was informed by an editor of a computer magazine about the writings of Alexander Mitschelich, of which I had known nothing. She advised that I read him carefully on the subject of "grief work," and I have done so. He argues that a culture, like a person, must endure a period of grief when there is a tragic loss. Failure to do so may lead to disorientation, self-hate, or even violence. My weeping friend meant to say that Germany has not yet done its grief work, and her elaborate review of man's inhumanities was a typical strategy of avoidance.

Mitschelich's name came up several times in my German travels, especially in conversations with professors, psychiatrists, sociologists, and journalists. But two other names were spoken (or implied) more often, much more often. As it turned out, together they provided me with a clearer understanding of the German situation, and why it is this *situation* and not the German *character* that is both fascinating and extremely dangerous.

The two names I am referring to are names of ideas. One of them is "America," and the other might be called "an unusable past." Although they were expressed in various ways during my conversations with intellectuals, these two ideas presented themselves in the clearest possible form on a street corner in Hamburg. A woman who represented herself as speaking for the Schiller Institute, and who was obviously a political propagandist, tried hard to convince me and others strolling in the street that West Germany must support "Star Wars" and other American military projects in order to "strengthen the West against the Russians, who are bent on European domination." A youth of about fifteen years of age came by and joined the conversation. He identified himself as an émigré from Russia, presently studying in Paris. Though he had given up his Russian passport for a French one, he denounced the woman's anti-Russian propaganda and offered some of his own. The Russians, he said, were not the problem. The Americans and their warlike imperialism were the true enemies of peace. I listened halfheartedly, which is the most one ought ever to do when confronted with ideologues. An important thought crossed my mind: I would be much better off partaking of some delicious Hamburg food than enduring this.

And then I observed an intense, ruddy-faced, sixty-year-old man about to join the conversation. It was not hard to sense his anger rising as first the pro-American propaganda was expressed and then the pro-Russian. When his face was nearing the color of a fresh matjes herring, he burst in with what may be called the "pro-German" case. The Russians, he said, are worse than Hitler, but the Americans are not very much better. They are vulgar and grasping, and have no sense of history. The Russians want to take Germany over but the Americans in fact have done so. A pox on both their houses. When I asked him to say exactly what the pro-German position implied, he was vague and became confused. He could provide no vision of Germany's future—not its political, cultural, or social future. What he called being "pro-German" was devoid of substance: his position was a name that referred to nothing. He began to sputter and wave his arms in a gesture of extreme frustration. And at this point, the question of the nature of Germany's present situation became clear to me. Everything I had been told and had seen came into sharp focus. Is there German schizophrenia? Yes, I concluded. And I felt I understood why. But—let me be explicit on this point—I did not know anything about the historical roots of my German Question. My journey did not tell me much about why Germany has had two faces for four hundred years, why Goethe and Goebbels could be produced by the same people. This I did not understand, do not, and perhaps never will. But I grasped what the affliction is now, in West Germany, and why it is dangerous.

West Germany is, in fact, the newest country in the Western world. It began in 1946, two years, ironically, before the establishment of the State of Israel. But unlike Israel, West Germany is devoid of a usable past. It is not just a new country, but a historically barren one. Germany's great cathedrals, universities, music, and literature are merely artifacts, objects fit for archeologists to study. They are of no use to modern-day Germans. For to use them, to refer to them, to revere them requires that one ask, What did they lead to? What spiritual inspiration did they give? What lessons did they teach? And the answers are devastating, for they led, in this century, to a twice-shattered culture that produced people who derived aesthetic pleasure from both Bach and Buchenwald. Germans know this better than anyone else. It is not, in the end, a question of hiding one's past from oneself or even of failing to do one's grief work. The Germans know their past—all of it—and have silently and reasonably concluded that it cannot be used as a guide to the future. Not now. Perhaps not for a century.

Thus, *Germany is terrified of itself*. Who would not be who cannot trust anything one has created? A journalist in Frankfurt told me that the most powerful carrier of the past, the German language itself, has become suspect. The word "Israeli" has replaced the word "Jew." "Volkdom" and "Aryan," even "Fatherland," can no longer be spoken seriously. Not only is much of the style and vocabulary of the Third Reich too frightening to be used in serious public discourse, even the traditional style of German abstruse thought is considered suspect.

A teacher of teachers from the University of Giessen told me that traditional German "humanistic" education is in disfavor. And when I asked a sociologist to comment on this, he said, "After all, Goebbels had a Ph.D. from the University of Heidelberg. Where does that kind of education lead?"

At a sermon at St. Katherina's Church in Frankfurt, I was astonished to hear a minister say that after Auschwitz, Christians were in no position to instruct Jews or indeed anyone else on how to interpret the Bible. Perhaps he was simply doing some grief work, but there was the distinct implication in his remarks that the religion that has sustained German culture for centuries is itself under suspicion.

A psychiatrist in Frankfurt told me that in his work with German patients the most common form of mental illness is "delusions of grandeur," but, significantly, very few believe they are Hitler or Kaiser Wilhelm or Frederick the Great or, indeed, any German at all. What should one make of this? In France, insane asylums have no shortage of Napoleons; in Britain, Henry the Eighths and Churchills can be found ruling the realm of the mad; and in America, our insane specialize in Jesus Christ (who we Americans tend to believe spoke English fluently and would have been an American if given half the chance). Apparently even the crazy in Germany find the past unusable.

But it is not the unusability of its past alone that creates a schizophrenic situation in Germany. A pathological paradox needs two unsupportable conditions. And America provides the second. To put it plainly, having no past, Germany has tried to provide itself with a future by adopting America's present. It is not important that West Germany was forced to do so after the war, that it was given no choice. Whatever the original conditions were, it is clear that Germany continues to be, and, out of desperation, wishes to be, conscious of itself only through the reflection of American culture.

I do not refer here to the American soldiers who are now as much a part of the German landscape as the Black Forest (and of the two, considering the extent of air pollution, are likely to remain longer). Or to the American air bases and cruise missiles. These are merely the artifacts of military alliance. I am referring to the living symbols of spiritual dependence, the massive intrusion of the American language and American films, fashions, food, music, style, iconography, design, credit cards, products, television, advertising. These have been swallowed whole as the antidote to a culture bereft of a trustworthy identity of its own. To paraphrase the legendary Viennese social critic Karl Kraus, this is the disease for which it claims to be the cure. For though it is intolerable for Germany to exist without guidelines from its own history, it is also intolerable for Germany to become Omaha, Nebraska. And the evidence for this is everywhere—if one listens with a "third ear."

A young taxi driver in Munich who is praised for his knowledge of English remarks that he learned much of it listening to American rock bands. "You can't do rock in the German language," he says. "So it's English or nothing." Though it is clear he cannot do without rock, he seems resentful and confused.

A psychiatrist in Karlsruhe says that German psychiatry takes all of its categories of mental illness from American psychiatry. "What we do is mostly what they do," he says. He adds that he does not know why this is so and insists that such a situation is unacceptable.

A publisher in Frankfurt complains that many American books are translated into German; few German books are translated into English. "We are more interested in what the Americans think than they are in what we think." He adds: "Are they interested in what anybody thinks?"

In Munich, a journalist who has lived and worked for

many years in Japan discourses on what he calls "the McDonald's culture." "The Japanese," he says, "can assimilate America. They can buy an American hamburger, take it home, and adapt it to their own traditions. They are a practical, malleable people. We cannot do this. With us, it must be one thing or another. If it is not the German way, then it will be the American way. One way or the other."

A waitress in Hamburg reports that she has never missed an episode of "Dynasty" (called "Denver" in Germany). But then adds, "It is trash."

Even in a traditional Bavarian beer garden, one senses both the presence of America and a contempt for it. To be sure, the waitresses still carry three mugs in each hand and the pretzels are elephantine. Nonetheless, the conversations, the cigarettes, the clothing have a distinctly American flavor. The folks from Omaha would feel quite at home here. When I mention this to an elderly man, he remarks that it used to be different, and then says no more.

But there is something darker, more sinister than all of this about the McDonald's culture and its fervid yet ambiguous reception in Germany. I heard it expressed, or thought I did, by intellectuals, and among the less articulate, it was alluded to in indirect, even indistinct ways. Not until I left Germany on a visit to Sweden did my third ear hear with clarity what had been whispered into it. In Sweden, I met a well-known editor, Arne Ruth, who, being unaware of my assignment in West Germany, nonetheless presented me with a copy of his book (written with Ingemar Karlsson). The book, which has been translated into German (but not English), is called *Society as Theater: Aesthetics and Politics in the Third Reich*. Its authors find the principal feature of the Third Reich to lie in a politics essentially without content; the Nazi regime, they contend, offers the ultimate example of politics as pure spectacle. The similarity between this thesis and my own in my last book, *Amusing Ourselves to Death,* was uncanny. In it I argued that American public discourse has been changed by the electronic media from serious exposition into a form of entertainment, and I concurred in the view of Aldous Huxley that in the future people might well be controlled by inflicting pleasure on them rather than pain. I even quoted Ronald Reagan's statement "Politics is show business." I would have felt comfortable entitling my book *Society as Theater.*

This coincidence of themes allowed me to see deeper than ever into the German dilemma. As Germans flee from the first terror—a culture without a past—they recoil from the second—an American culture that offers them intimations and shadows of that which ruined them. I do not say that America today is in most respects like Germany in the 1930s, and I do not believe that America is capable of producing an Auschwitz. But the point is that the Germans do not know this. They sense that they have imported a culture with little intellectual coherence, uninterested in its own traditions, and preoccupied with the creation of spectacle. Even those who adore Ronald Reagan (and with few exceptions TMOS told me they do) know that he is incapable of conceiving and putting together five consecutive sentences of political substance and logical force. He is a good image for his country, Germans told me. He is not afraid of the Russians and hates Communists. He encourages optimism and confidence. He is an aesthetic delight. Whom does that remind you of? What does that remind you of? I am sure that Germans know the answers (even if Americans do not) and they are disgusted by them.

Does this situation make Germany dangerous? I should think it does. A culture that is frightened at looking back and contemptuous of the only future that seems to lie ahead must always be considered dangerous. As to when and where and to whom, I do not know. But this much can be said: there can be no laying the past to rest, no embarking on a creative future, no peace of mind as long as the twin nemeses of dread and loathing hover over Germany.

A Muted
Celebration

*Asked by an editor in 1986 to take notice in some fashion
of the two-hundredth anniversary of* The Columbian, *I
took the opportunity to immerse myself in the history of
magazines. As you will see,* The Columbian's *claim to be
the first general-interest modern-style magazine is prob-
lematic, which is one reason why I entitled my essay "A
Muted Celebration." Another reason is that the future of
such magazines is cloudy, and to avoid the impression of
overconfidence one must keep the celebration quiet and
dignified.*

orton Zuckerman, the owner of *The Atlantic*, is interviewed by *New York Newsday*. George Steiner,
the eminent literary scholar, delivers the R. R.
Bowker Memorial Lecture. The events do not occur at the
same time, and the remarks of each man are offered with
quite different intentions. Nonetheless, when juxtaposed,
they provide us with a short but provocative dialogue on the
state of the general magazine in America and, therefore, on
the state of literacy.

After conceding that *The Atlantic* is not making money,
as he had predicted it would, Zuckerman was asked, "Do

you think there is a future for *The Atlantic* and similar literate, general-interest magazines?" Zuckerman replied: "I do. There are an increasing number of people who are well educated, and who are used to receiving ideas in print. It's not necessarily the largest audience, but at least it's an extremely active, educated, involved audience. I think there will always be such an audience." Why Zuckerman believes this, he did not say. For all their talk about bottom lines, businessmen live off the largesse of hope as much as the rest of us. Perhaps—to be fair to him—he meant his last statement to be a question rather than an assertion. He would certainly have abjured certainty had he read Steiner's Bowker Lecture.

As if responding to Zuckerman's entrepreneurial optimism, Steiner hypothesized that we have come to the end of that period of time in which there are enough serious readers to sustain publications like *The Atlantic*. He argued that in the eighteenth century a revolution in the structure of the arts of reading commenced. It was characterized by the rise of the book as a mass medium, the emergence of public libraries, and the development of the general-interest periodical. As a consequence, there came into being a happy relationship between the best that was thought and written, and a mass audience prepared and eager to read it. That relationship broke down, he believes, in the first two decades of the twentieth century, so that reading in the sense that Erasmus or Balzac or Jefferson or even Mark Twain would have understood the word is no longer an activity of the masses. "I would conjecture," Steiner remarked, "that the period, let us say, from the French Revolution to the catastrophes of world war marks an oasis, an oasis of quality, in which very great literature, very great non-fiction did reach a mass audience."

Steiner believes we have now passed through the oasis and reentered the desert, with the result that we shall be left with three kinds of reading. The first is reading for distraction—which is what makes the airport book so popular. The second is reading for information—which comes to mind when one is confronted by such terms as "computer print-out," "microcircuit," and "teletext." The third kind of reading is a residue of the great age of literacy, now receding rapidly under the compulsions of the Age of Information. It requires silence, patience, a ready capacity for reflection, the training to be challenged by complexity and, above all, a willingness to suspend the distractions of the world so that reader and text may become a unity of time, space, and imagination. For our purposes, we may call this kind of reading Zuckerman's Hope, for the future of the literate, general-interest magazine depends entirely on there being enough readers in this third sense. Against Zuckerman's Hope, there is Steiner's Prophecy, which he expressed with an ominous briskness: "What about reading in the old, archaic, private, silent sense? This may become as specialized a skill and avocation as it was in the *scriptoria* and libraries of the monasteries during the so-called Dark Ages."

Thus, in commemorating the two-hundredth anniversary of America's first genuine magazine, *The Columbian,* one proceeds with a sense of gloomy uncertainty. Is one writing a eulogy for magazines? That is not my intention. I come to praise, not to bury. Nonetheless, the specter of obsolescence will not go away. This must be a muted celebration.

Moreover, as there is uncertainty about the future of the magazine, there is uncertainty about its past as well. We settle upon the publication of *The Columbian* in 1786 as America's first magazine in the same way that we settle upon Gutenberg's Bible in 1456 as the beginning of the printed book— which is to say, as a matter of convenience. Everything depends, of course, on how we define our terms. The word "magazine" comes from the French *magasin,* which means "storehouse" (as every sailor knows). The earliest magazines in England and on the Continent were, indeed, storage places for sketches, verse, essays, and miscellany. To most eighteenth-century readers, the word "magazine" meant miscellany, and was not necessarily positive. In one of his notes to *The Dunciad,* Alexander Pope defined magazines as "upstart collections" of dullness and folly. To the present day, the word retains a residual connotation of entertainment or, worse, triviality. As Frank Luther Mott, the dean of magazine historians, points out, a professional and technical publication for psychiatrists would disdain calling itself *The Psychiatrists' Magazine* and choose instead *The Psychiatrists' Journal* or *Review.*

Nonetheless, some of the most eminent names of eighteenth-century English literature are associated with what, for want of a better word, we would be inclined to call magazines. For example, in 1704, before he wrote *Robinson Crusoe* and *Moll Flanders,* Daniel Defoe brought out what is generally taken to be the first British magazine, *The Review* (later known as *Defoe's Review*). Richard Steele started *The Tatler* in 1709, and in 1711 joined with Joseph Addison in publishing the first issue of the famous *Spectator.* Even Alexander Pope got into the act, for he wrote for and may have founded *The Grub Street Journal,* which lasted from 1730 to 1738. For those who believe the name is the thing, however, we must acknowledge that the first publication ever to bear the name "magazine" was brought out in 1731 by Edward Cave, a London printer and bookseller, who called his product *Gentleman's Magazine.* In his introduction to Volume I, he described its contents thus: "a Monthly collection, to treasure up, as in a Magazine, the most remarkable Pieces on the subjects abovementioned, or at least impartial abridgements thereof." The word "abridgements" is important, since Cave was largely concerned at the start to provide outlines of the best material appearing in the journals of the day (and thus anticipated by two hundred years the purported mission of *The Reader's Digest*). However, soon after publication, Cave extended his scope to include prose and verse, historical and biographical sketches, obituaries, listings of other publications, songs (both music and lyrics, a tradition *The Ladies' Home Journal* would continue later), engravings and maps, and reports of debates in Parliament. This last section was written by one of the magazine's contributors, Dr. Samuel Johnson. From sketchy notes and his own articulate imagination, Johnson wrote the speeches he attributed to the English statesmen of the day, thus elevating the quality of both the speeches and the speakers.

By 1744, *Gentleman's Magazine* reached a circulation of 10,000 readers, not a few of whom lived in America. It was inevitable, therefore, that the Americans would generate some home-grown products of their own, using *Gentleman's Magazine* as a model. It will surprise no one that the first *plan* for an American magazine was conceived by Benjamin Franklin. But he was slow, by three days, in making it the first reality. Andrew Bradford issued his *American Magazine, or A Monthly View of the Political State of the British Colonies,* on February 13, 1741. Franklin's *General Magazine and Historical Chronicle for All the British Plantations in America* appeared on February 16. Bradford's magazine lasted three months, Franklin's six. But a start had been made and a pattern set. From 1741 to 1800, forty-five magazines were founded in America. Sixty percent of them did not last through their first year. Four died after one month; only four reached the age of three years. But among them there were some impressive specimens, particularly William Bradford's *The American Magazine and Monthly Chronicle,* which began in 1759 and lasted for thirteen months.

Why, then, do we celebrate *The Columbian,* which did not appear until September 1786, as our first true general magazine? The case is largely based on four considerations. First, it was the first publication whose form is clearly recognizable to us as a magazine. Through most of the eighteenth century, a magazine was distinguished by its content, not its format, and the pre-*Columbian* magazines had the look of the newspapers and pamphlets of the time. Their paper was of rough rag stock, their covers of a flimsier colored stock, the type like that of newspapers. *The Columbian* not only used smaller type but was presented in a format vaguely reminiscent today of *The New Yorker*. In short, it gave to magazines the shape of things to come.

Second, *The Columbian* was issued at approximately the same time every month for eight years (until a change in postal regulations made delivery too costly to continue); that is to say, the regularity of its distribution was similar to that of modern magazines. Third, it largely disdained the reprinting of newspaper articles, book excerpts, and speeches. Instead, it solicited both fiction and non-fiction from individual writers and paid them for their contributions, a practice virtually unheard of at the time. It treated writers with high regard, and did not usually require them to alter either their substance or their style to fit the editor's inclinations. To use the parlance of today, *The Columbian* was the first "writer's book."

And finally, a case can be made that its editor, Mathew Carey, established many of the traditions that up to the present time govern the conduct of magazine editors. Carey was an Irish expatriate who had spent time in prison for his essays denouncing the power of the Church of England. He worked briefly for Benjamin Franklin when he came to America, and until he was badly wounded in a duel produced a newspaper called *The Pennsylvania Herald*. In 1786, he joined with William Spotswood and James Trenchard to produce *The Columbian*, whose intention, they announced, was to capture "the new spirit of the new America," a sufficiently vague commitment to give Carey the scope he needed to develop his ideas about editing. For example, although Carey was an ardent anti-Federalist, he did not regard *The Columbian* as an instrument of anti-Federalist opinion. From its beginning, he published a number of superior Federalist writings (in contrast to one of its principal competitors, Noah Webster's *The American Magazine,* which single-mindedly printed only those arguments in favor of Federalism). In a sense, Carey freed the magazine from the shackles of political ideology. He also pioneered the idea of a writer's ownership of his own material. (So did Noah Webster.) And, unlike most editors of the time, including Webster, Carey wrote nothing himself. He conveyed his vision through the selection of material produced by others. (Toward the end of 1787, when Carey became the publisher of *The American Museum,* he not only hired Francis Hopkinson to be his paid editor but also hired the essayist Jeremy Belknap as a staff writer, the first paid staff writer in American magazine history.)

And so, though argument to the contrary must be allowed, we hail the bicentennial of *The Columbian* as representing the beginnings of a rich literary tradition. Even a rough review of that tradition reveals that through most of the nineteenth century American literature was, as much as anything else, a *magazine* literature. Consider the list of contributors to *The Saturday Evening Post,* founded in 1821, which includes William Cullen Bryant, Harriet Beecher Stowe, James Fenimore Cooper, Ralph Waldo Emerson, Nathaniel Hawthorne, and Edgar Allan Poe—in other words, most of the writers included in American Lit. 101. Emerson, Thoreau, and Margaret Fuller served as joint editors of the literary magazine *The Dial,* which lasted from 1840 to 1844. John Greenleaf Whittier edited *National Era,* which in 1852 printed *Uncle Tom's Cabin* in its entirety. James Russell Lowell became the first editor of *The Atlantic Monthly* in 1857.

Harper's (of which there were several incarnations) was founded in 1850, *The Nation* in 1865. Together they provided a forum for every major writer in America. Even the women's magazines which began to flourish in the 1880s and 1890s—*McCall's, Ladies' Home Journal, Good Housekeeping, Cosmopolitan,* and *Collier's*—featured impressive literary figures. *The Delineator,* a women's magazine founded near the end of the nineteenth century, was edited by Theodore Dreiser. And one must not omit mentioning Sara Josepha Hale, who as early as 1832 founded *Ladies Magazine* and who made an enduring contribution to American literature by writing the poem "Mary Had a Little Lamb."

In addition to providing both a shape to and an outlet for the development of American literature, the nineteenth-century magazine made another important contribution to American culture, a contribution from which we have not yet recovered and perhaps never will: magazines created the advertising industry. Although magazine advertising was not unknown before the 1880s, the situation changed drastically when Congress passed the Postal Act of March 3, 1879, which gave magazines low-cost mailing privileges. As a consequence, they emerged as the best available conduits for national advertising. To give one example of how quickly both magazines and merchants seized their opportunities, the November 12, 1885, issue of *The Independent* ran ads for the following products and services: peas, baking powder, bikes, glue, R. H. Macy & Co., life insurance, pianos, rail travel, boots, picket fences, reversible collars, cuffs, cures for deafness, and the Grand Union Hotel in Saratoga Springs. Such advertising not only made the names of companies well known but also changed methods of manufacturing and distribution. Consumers turned away from home-made and local products and toward mass-produced, national brands sold to the largest possible market. When George Eastman invented the portable camera in 1888, he spent $25,000 advertising it in magazines. By 1895, "Kodak" and "camera" were synonymous, as to some extent they still are. Companies like Royal Baking Powder, Baker's Chocolate, Ivory Soap, and Gillette moved into a national market by advertising their products in magazines. Even magazines moved into a national market by advertising themselves in magazines, the most conspicuous example being *Ladies' Home Journal*. Its publisher, Cyrus H. K. Curtis, spent half a million dollars between 1883 and 1888 advertising his magazine in other magazines. By 1909, *Ladies' Home Journal* had a circulation of over 1 million readers.

Curtis's enthusiasm for advertising notwithstanding, the most significant figure in mating advertising to the magazine was Frank Munsey, who upon his death in 1925 was eulogized by William Allen White with the following words: "Frank Munsey contributed to the journalism of his day the talent of a meat packer, the morals of a money changer and the manners of an undertaker. He and his kind have about succeeded in transforming a once-noble profession into an 8% security. May he rest in trust." What was the sin of the malevolent Munsey? Simply, he made two discoveries. First, a large circulation could be achieved by selling a magazine for much less than it cost to produce; and, second, huge profits could be made from the high volume of advertising that a large circulation would attract. In October 1893, Munsey took out an ad in *The New York Sun* announcing that *Munsey's Magazine* was cutting its price from 25 cents to 10 cents, and reducing a year's subscription from $3 to $1. The first 10-cent issue claimed a circulation of 40,000; within four months, the circulation rose to 200,000; two months later, it was 500,000. Although *Munsey's* was filled with pulp writing, his discoveries about how to conduct the business of magazines established the pattern for all magazines. In 1900,

Harper's contained more advertising than it had carried in all its preceding twenty-two years.

With national advertising as its economic base, with a tradition of publishing the best being thought and written, and with a large, receptive readership, the magazine soared to new heights in the early years of this century. In the pages of *The Smart Set, American Mercury, The New Yorker, The Saturday Review of Literature, Harper's, The Atlantic Monthly, Vanity Fair, The Nation,* and *The New Republic,* American prose—both fiction and non-fiction—sang with an unprecedented vibrancy and intensity. Who would have dared to say then that this was a nightingale's song, most brilliant and sweet as the singer nears the moment of death? Indeed, even now one holds back from saying it. But there is no denying that underneath the melody, some new notes were sounding, playing a new kind of tune that would bring down the curtain—not perhaps on the general magazine but on its days of glory.

What happened was the electric plug, to which were attached media of great variety and allure, all of them attacking the prestige, economics, and monopoly of the literate, general-interest magazine. Together, radio, movies, and television—"the media," as they have become known—assaulted magazines from several different directions. First, they undermined their economic base by robbing them of advertising revenues. In 1950, for example, $515 million was spent on magazine advertising, or 9 percent of all advertising expenditures, and only $171 million, or 3 percent, was spent on television. By 1966, $1.295 billion was spent on magazines (7.8 percent) and $2.765 billion for television (16.7 percent). This trend has continued unabated. Radio also played a part in reducing magazine revenues, as did movies. Movies, of course, did not compete directly for advertising money but, instead, took a piece of the money and time people normally spent on other leisure activities.

The second, related point is that the media altered the structure of leisure activities. Radio, for example, made it unnecessary for people to read to each other, or to read at all. Movies led people out of their homes; television brought them back but not to read. At the present time, approximately 90 million Americans are watching television every night during prime-time hours. "Watching television" is something quite different from "watching a television program." The latter implies a selection, the former a compulsion. The point is worth making because to some extent the general magazine addressed itself to an audience of compulsive readers, now replaced by compulsive screen watchers. Moreover, the availability of a variety of media (including the stereo and the much-underestimated telephone) altered both the sound and distraction levels of the average home so that conditions for serious reading were degraded.

Third, movies and television, aided by the development of photography, helped to create a visual culture. To a great extent, the picture has replaced the word as the central mode of public discourse in America. Politicians, ministers, journalists, and judges are now known by their faces, not their words. Even worse, audiences have grown accustomed to receiving information in the form of images—indeed, rapidly moving images—and no longer have the patience or possibly the ability to process the fixed, lineal, abstract word. Moreover, the instantaneity of speed-of-light media has made the printed word seem obsolescent. Not only is yesterday's newspaper old news but so is today's newspaper.

And finally, the media have drawn to themselves much of the talent that in an earlier time would have devoted itself to writing for magazines. Writing screenplays and television sit-coms holds the promise of a degree of fame and fortune with which magazine writing cannot compete. And so, as readers abandon the form as too complex or too slow or too out-of-date, writers abandon the form as too low-paying or too limited in audience.

Where do we go from here? Eulogies, one hopes, are premature. For one thing, some magazines have changed their form to accommodate the new role of reading in people's lives. *Harper's,* for example, has reduced the length of its stories and articles to suit its readers' impaired capacity for sustained concentration. For another, there is some accumulating evidence that for many products print advertising is more effective than television advertising. The corporate world does not yet quite believe this, but should it be persuaded, the economic base of magazines would be significantly strengthened. Third, the spread of both illiteracy and aliteracy (the ability without the inclination to read) has, at long last, become visible as a national crisis. Educators and legislators have begun to offer solutions that may in the long run give substance to Zuckerman's Hope. George Steiner himself has suggested that we convert all our undergraduate colleges into *schools of reading.* There is even a cadre of educators (among whom I include myself) who would carry Steiner's proposal to the high school. And, of course, changes in the structure of education may yet do much to restore the importance of the printed word. There is nothing far-fetched about this possibility. After all, changes in the structure of education in the seventeenth and eighteenth centuries contributed enormously to the prestige and power of the printed word.

And finally, we may draw a small measure of optimism from the fact that there is no result of media change so inevitable that we can speak with certainty of the future. The study of media history reveals—time and again—that there are always surprises in store. Those who make predictions—

either giddy or somber—about the demise of serious forms of literature may turn out to be quite wrong. Here, uncertainty is our friend. And so, with full appreciation of the struggle that the general-interest magazine is now engaged in, we may raise our colors in its behalf by honoring its two-hundredth birthday and telling our young of its robust history. And, of course, by not failing to renew our subscriptions.

The Parable of the Ring Around the Collar

This and the following essay are among several in this book dealing with television. Their purpose is the same: to shed light on the relationship between the form and the social consequences of certain kinds of television programs. It is worth noting here that one difference between Americans and Europeans is that the latter take television seriously. Europeans seem to understand that media change is ecological, not additive; that when a powerful new medium like television enters a culture, the result is not the old culture plus the new medium, but a new culture altogether. The effect is similar to what happens if you add a drop of red dye to a beaker of clear water: you end up with a new color throughout. I have been close to obsessed about television, for it does not seem to me that my countrymen have yet taken its measure. We speak about America as if television has merely been added to it and little else has changed. Americans watch television, but we have not yet reached the point where we watch ourselves watch it.

Television commercials are a form of religious literature. To comment on them in a serious vein is to practice hermeneutics, the branch of theology concerned with interpreting and explaining the Scriptures. This is what I propose to do here. The heathens, heretics, and unbelievers may move on to something else.

I do not claim, for a start, that every television commercial has religious content. Just as in church the pastor will sometimes call the congregation's attention to non-ecclesiastical matters, so there are television commercials that are entirely secular. Someone has something to sell; you are told what it is, where it can be obtained, and what it costs. Though these may be shrill and offensive, no doctrine is advanced and no theology invoked.

But the majority of important television commercials take the form of religious parables organized around a coherent theology. Like all religious parables, they put forward a concept of sin, intimations of the way to redemption, and a vision of Heaven. They also suggest what are the roots of evil and what are the obligations of the holy.

Consider, for example, the Parable of the Ring Around the Collar. This is to television scripture what the Parable of the Prodigal Son is to the Bible, which is to say it is an archetype containing most of the elements of form and content that recur in its genre. To begin with, the Parable of the Ring Around the Collar is short, occupying only about thirty seconds of one's time and attention. There are three reasons for this, all obvious. First, it is expensive to preach on television; second, the attention span of the congregation is not long and is highly vulnerable to distraction; and third, a parable does not need to be long—tradition dictating that its narrative structure be tight, its symbols unambiguous, its explication terse.

The narrative structure of the Parable of the Ring Around the Collar is, indeed, comfortably traditional. The story has a beginning, a middle, and an end. A married couple is depicted in some relaxed setting—a restaurant, say—in which they are enjoying each other's company and generally having a wonderful time. But then a waitress approaches their table, notices that the man has a dirty collar, stares at it boldly, sneers with cold contempt, and announces to all within hearing the nature of his transgression. The man is humiliated and glares at his wife with scorn, for she is the source of his shame. She, in turn, assumes an expression of self-loathing mixed with a touch of self-pity. This is the parable's beginning: the presentation of the problem.

The parable continues by showing the wife at home using a detergent that never fails to eliminate dirt around the collars of men's shirts. She proudly shows her husband what she is doing, and he forgives her with an adoring smile. This is the parable's middle: the solution of the problem. Finally, we are shown the couple in a restaurant once again, but this time they are free of the waitress's probing eyes and bitter social chastisement. This is the parable's end: the moral, the explication, the exegesis. From this, we should draw the proper conclusion.

As in all parables, behind the apparent simplicity there are some profound ideas to ponder. Among the most subtle and important is the notion of where and how problems originate. Embedded in every belief system there is an assumption about the root cause of evil from which the varieties of sinning take form. In science, for example, evil is represented in superstition. In psychoanalysis, we find it in early, neurotic transactions with our parents. In Christianity, it is located in the concept of Original Sin.

In television-commercial parables, the root cause of evil is Technological Innocence, a failure to know the particulars of the beneficent accomplishments of industrial progress. This is the primary source of unhappiness, humiliation, and discord in life. And, as forcefully depicted in the Parable of the Ring, the consequences of technological innocence may strike at any time, without warning, and with the full force of their disintegrating action.

The sudden striking power of technological innocence is a particularly important feature of television-commercial theology, for it is a constant reminder of the congregation's vulnerability. One must never be complacent or, worse, self-congratulatory. To attempt to live without technological sophistication is at all times dangerous, since the evidence of one's naïveté will always be painfully visible to the vigilant. The vigilant may be a waitress, a friend, a neighbor, or even a spectral figure—a holy ghost, as it were—who materializes in your kitchen, from nowhere, to give witness to your sluggardly ignorance.

Technological innocence refers not only to ignorance of detergents, drugs, sanitary napkins, cars, salves, and foodstuffs, but also to ignorance of technical machinery such as savings banks and transportation systems. One may, for example, come upon one's neighbors while on vacation (in television-commercial parables, this is always a sign of danger) and discover that they have invested their money in a certain bank of whose special interest rates you have been unaware. This is, of course, a moral disaster, and both you and your vacation are doomed.

As demonstrated in the Ring Parable, there is a path to redemption, but it can be entered only on two conditions. The first requires that you be open to advice or social criticism from those who are more enlightened. In the Ring Parable, the waitress serves the function of counselor, although she is, to be sure, exacting and very close to unforgiving. In some parables, the adviser is rather more sarcastic than severe. But in most parables, as for example in all sanitary napkin, mouthwash, shampoo, and aspirin commercials, the advisers are amiable and sympathetic, perhaps all too aware of their own vulnerability on other matters.

The Innocent are required to accept instruction in the spirit in which it is offered. This cannot be stressed enough, for it instructs the congregation in two lessons simultaneously: one must be eager to accept advice, and just as eager to give it. Giving advice is, so to speak, the principal obligation of the holy. In fact, the ideal religious community may be depicted in images of dozens of people, each in his or her turn giving and taking advice on technological advances.

The second condition involves one's willingness to act on the advice given. As in traditional Christian theology, it is not sufficient to hear the gospel or even preach it. One's understanding must be expressed in good works. In the Ring Parable, the once-pitiable wife acts almost immediately, and the parable concludes by showing the congregation the effects of her action. In the Parable of the Person with Rotten Breath, of which there are several versions, we are shown a woman who, ignorant of the technological solution to her problem, is enlightened by a supportive roommate. The woman takes the advice without delay, with results we are shown in the last five seconds: a honeymoon in Hawaii. In the Parable of the Stupid Investor, we are shown a man who knows not how to make his money make money. Upon enlightenment, he acts swiftly and, at the parable's end, he is rewarded with a car, or a trip to Hawaii, or something approximating peace of mind.

Because of the compactness of commercial parables, the ending—that is, the last five seconds—must serve a dual purpose. It is, of course, the moral of the story: if one will act in such a way, this will be the reward. But in being shown the result, we are also shown an image of Heaven. Occasionally, as in the Parable of the Lost Traveler's Checks, we are given a glimpse of Hell: Technological Innocents lost and condemned to eternal wandering far from their native land. But mostly we are given images of a Heaven both accessible and delicious: that is, a Heaven that is here, now, on earth, in America, and quite often in Hawaii.

But Hawaii is only a convenient recurring symbol. Heaven can, in fact, materialize and envelop you anywhere. In the Parable of the Man Who Runs Through Airports, Heaven is found at a car-rental counter to which the confounded Runner is shepherded by an angelic messenger. The expression of ecstasy on the Runner's face tells clearly that this moment is as close to transcendence as he can ever hope for.

Ecstasy is the key idea here, for commercial parables depict the varieties of ecstasy in as much detail as you will find in any body of religious literature. At the conclusion of the Parable of the Spotted Glassware, a husband and wife assume such ecstatic countenances as can only be described by the word "beatification." Even in the Ring Parable, which at first glance would not seem to pose as serious a moral crisis as spotted glassware, we are shown ecstasy, pure and serene. And where ecstasy is, so is Heaven. Heaven, in brief, is any place where you have joined your soul with the Deity—the Deity, of course, being Technology.

Just when, as a religious people, we replaced our faith in traditional ideas of God with a belief in the ennobling force of Technology is not easy to say. Television commercials played no role in bringing about this transformation, but they reflect the change, document it, and amplify it. They constitute the most abundant literature we possess of our new spiritual commitment. That is why we have a solemn obligation to keep television commercials under the continuous scrutiny of hermeneutics.

The News

The whole problem with news on television comes down to this: all the words uttered in an hour of news coverage could be printed on one page of a newspaper. And the world cannot be understood in one page. Of course, there is a compensation: television offers pictures, and the pictures move. It is often said that moving pictures are a kind of language in themselves, and there is a good deal of truth in this. But the language of pictures differs radically from oral and written language, and the differences are crucial for understanding television news.

To begin with, the grammar of pictures is weak in communicating past-ness and present-ness. When terrorists want to prove to the world that their kidnap victims are still alive, they photograph them holding a copy of a recent newspaper. The dateline on the newspaper provides the proof that the photograph was taken on or after that date. Without the help of the written word, film and videotape cannot portray temporal dimensions with any precision. Consider a film clip showing an aircraft carrier at sea. One might be able to identify the ship as Soviet or American, but there would be no way of telling where in the world the carrier was, where it was headed, or when the pictures were taken. It is only through language—words spoken over the pictures or reproduced in them—that the image of the aircraft carrier takes on meaning as a portrayal of a specific event.

Still, it is possible to enjoy the image of the carrier for its own sake. One might find the hugeness of the vessel interesting; it signifies military power on the move. There is a certain drama in watching the planes come in at high speeds and skid to a stop on the deck. Suppose the ship were burning: that would be even more interesting. This leads to a second point about the language of pictures. The grammar of moving pictures favors images that change. That is why violence and destruction find their way onto television so often. When something is destroyed violently its constitution is altered in a highly visible way: hence the entrancing power of fire. Fire gives visual form to the ideas of consumption, disappearance, death—the thing which is burned is actually taken away by fire. It is at this very basic level that fires make a good subject for television news. Something was here, now it's gone, and the change is recorded on film.

Earthquakes and typhoons have the same power: before the viewer's eyes the world is taken apart. If a television viewer has relatives in Mexico City and an earthquake occurs there, then she may take an interest in the images of destruction as a report from a specific place and time. That is, she may look to television news for information about an important event. But film of an earthquake can still be interesting if the viewer cares nothing about the event itself. Which is only to say that there is another way of participating in the news—as a spectator who desires to be entertained. Actually to see buildings topple is exciting, no matter where the buildings are. The world turns to dust before our eyes.

Those who produce television news in America know that their medium favors images that move. That is why they despise "talking heads," people who simply appear in front of a camera and speak. When talking heads appear on television, there is nothing to record or document, no change in process. In the cinema the situation is somewhat different. On a movie screen, close-ups of a good actor speaking dramatically can sometimes be interesting to watch. When Clint Eastwood narrows his eyes and challenges his rival to shoot first, the spectator sees the cool rage of the Eastwood character take visual form, and the narrowing of the eyes is dramatic. But much of the effect of this small movement depends on the size of the movie screen and the darkness of the theater, which make Eastwood and his every action "larger than life."

The television screen is smaller than life. It occupies about 15 percent of the viewer's visual field (compared to about 70 percent for the movie screen). It is not set in a darkened theater closed off from the world but in the viewer's ordinary living space. This means that visual changes must be more extreme and more dramatic to be interesting on television. A narrowing of the eyes will not do. A car crash, an earthquake, a burning factory are much better.

With these principles in mind, let us examine more closely the structure of a typical newscast. In America, almost all news shows begin with music, the tone of which suggests important events about to unfold. (Beethoven's Fifth Symphony would be entirely appropriate.) The music is very important, for it equates the news with various forms of drama and ritual—the opera, for example, or a wedding procession—in which musical themes underscore the meaning of the event. Music takes us immediately into the realm of the symbolic, a world that is not to be taken literally. After all, when events unfold in the real world, they do so without musical accompaniment. More symbolism follows. The sound of teletype machines can be heard in the studio, not because it is impossible to screen this noise out, but because the sound is a kind of music in itself. It tells us that data are pouring in from all corners of the globe, a sensation reinforced by the world map in the background (or clocks noting the time on different continents).

Already, then, before a single news item is introduced, a great deal has been communicated. We know that we are in the presence of a symbolic event, a form of theater in which the day's events are to be dramatized. This theater takes the entire globe as its subject, although it may look at the world from the perspective of a single nation. A certain tension is present, like the atmosphere in a theater just before the curtain goes up. The tension is represented by the music, the staccato beat of the teletype machines, and the sight of newsworkers scurrying around typing reports and answering phones. As a technical matter, it would be no problem to build a set in which the newsroom staff remained off camera, invisible to the viewer, but an important theatrical effect would be lost. By being busy on camera, the workers help communicate urgency about the events at hand, which it is suggested are changing so rapidly that constant revision of the news is necessary.

The staff in the background also helps signal the importance of the person in the center, the anchorman (or -woman) "in command" of both the staff and the news. The anchorman plays the role of host. He welcomes us to the newscast and welcomes us back from the different locations we visit during filmed reports. His voice, appearance, and manner establish the mood of the broadcast. It would be unthinkable for the anchor to be ugly, or a nervous sort who could not complete a sentence. Viewers must be able to believe in the anchor as a person of authority and skill, a person who would not panic in a crisis—someone to trust.

This belief is based not on knowledge of the anchorman's character or achievements as a journalist, but on his presentation of self while on the air. Does he look the part of a trusted man? Does he speak firmly and clearly? Does he have a warm smile? Does he project confidence without seeming arrogant? The value the anchor must communicate above all else is control. He must be in control of himself, his voice, his emotions. He must know what is coming next in the broadcast, and he must move smoothly and confidently from segment to segment. Again, it would be unthinkable for the anchor to break down and weep over a story, or laugh uncontrollably on camera, no matter how "human" these responses may be.

Many other features of the newscast help the anchor to establish the impression of control. These are usually equated with professionalism in broadcasting. They include such things as graphics that tell the viewer what is being shown, or maps and charts that suddenly appear on the screen and disappear on cue, or the orderly progression from story to story, starting with the most important events first. They also include the absence of gaps or "deadtime" during the broadcast, even the simple fact that the news starts and ends at a certain hour. These common features are thought of as purely technical matters, which a professional crew handles as a matter of course. But they are also symbols of a dominant theme of television news: the imposition of an orderly world—called "the news"—upon the disorderly flow of events.

While the form of a news broadcast emphasizes tidiness and control, its content can best be described as chaotic. Because time is so precious on television, because the nature of the medium favors dynamic visual images, and because the pressures of a commercial structure require the news to hold its audience above all else, there is rarely any attempt to explain issues in depth or place events in their proper context. The news moves nervously from a warehouse fire to a court decision, from a guerrilla war to a World Cup match, the quality of the film often determining the length of the story. Certain stories show up only because they offer dramatic pictures. Bleachers collapse in South America: hundreds of people are crushed—a perfect television news story, for the cameras can record the face of disaster in all its anguish. Back in Washington, a new budget is approved by Congress. Here there is nothing to photograph because a budget is not a physical event; it is a document full of language and numbers. So the producers of the news will show a photo of the document itself, focusing on the cover where it says: "Budget of the United States of America." Or sometimes they will send a camera crew to the government printing plant where copies of the budget are produced. That evening, while the contents of the budget are summarized by a voice-over, the viewer sees stacks of documents being loaded into boxes at the government printing plant. Then a few of the budget's more important provisions will be flashed on the screen in written form, but this is such a time-consuming process—using television as a printed page—that the producers keep it to a minimum. In short, the budget is not televisable, and for that reason its time on the news must be brief. The bleacher collapse will get more minutes that evening.

With priorities of this sort, it is almost impossible for the news to offer an adequate account of important events. Indeed, it is the trivial event that is often best suited for television coverage. This is such a commonplace that no one even bothers to challenge it. Walter Cronkite, a revered figure in television and anchorman of the CBS Evening News for many years, has acknowledged several times that television cannot be relied on to inform the citizens of a democratic nation.

Unless they also read newspapers and magazines, television viewers are helpless to understand their world, Cronkite has said. No one at CBS has ever disagreed with his conclusion, other than to say, "We do the best we can."

Of course, it is a tendency of journalism in general to concentrate on the surface of events rather than underlying conditions; this is as true for the newspaper as it is for the newscast. But several features of television undermine whatever efforts journalists may make to give sense to the world. One is that a television broadcast is a series of events that occur in sequence, and the sequence is the same for all viewers. This is not true for a newspaper page, which displays many items simultaneously, allowing readers to choose the order in which they read them. If a newspaper reader wants only a summary of the latest tax bill, he can read the headline and the first paragraph of an article, and if he wants more, he can keep reading. In a sense, then, everyone reads a different newspaper, for no two readers will read (or ignore) the same items.

But all television viewers see the same broadcast. They have no choices. A report is either in the broadcast or out, which means that anything which is of narrow interest is unlikely to be included. As NBC News executive Reuven Frank once explained:

> A newspaper, for example, can easily afford to print an item of conceivable interest to only a fraction of its readers. A television news program must be put together with the assumption that each item will be of some interest to everyone that watches. Every time a newspaper includes a feature which will attract a specialized group it can assume it is adding at least a little bit to its circulation. To the degree a television news program includes an item

of this sort . . . it must assume that its audience will diminish.

The need to "include everyone," an identifying feature of commercial television in all its forms, prevents journalists from offering lengthy or complex explanations, or from tracing the sequence of events leading up to today's headlines. One of the ironies of political life in modern democracies is that many problems which concern the "general welfare" are of interest only to specialized groups. Arms control, for example, is an issue that literally concerns everyone in the world, and yet the language of arms control and the complexity of the subject are so daunting that only a minority of people can actually follow the issue from week to week and month to month. If it wants to act responsibly, a newspaper can at least make available more information about arms control than most people want. But commercial television cannot afford to do so.

This illustrates an important point in the psychology of television's appeal. Many of the items in newspapers and magazines are not, in a strict sense, demanded by a majority of readers. They are there because some readers *might* be interested or because the editors think their readers *should* be interested. On commercial television, "might" and "should" are not the relevant words. The producers attempt to make sure that "each item will be of some interest to everyone that watches," as Reuven Frank put it. What this means is that a newspaper or magazine can challenge its audience in a way that television cannot. Print media have the luxury of suggesting or inviting interest, whereas television must always concern itself with conforming to existing interests. In a way, television is more strictly responsive to the demands of its huge audience. But there is one demand it cannot meet: the desire to be challenged, to be told "this is worth attending to," to be surprised by what one thought would not be of interest.

Another severe limitation on television is time. There is simply not enough of it. The evening news programs at CBS, NBC, and ABC all run for thirty minutes, eight of which are taken up by commercials. No one believes that twenty-two minutes for the day's news is adequate. For years news executives at ABC, NBC, and CBS have suggested that the news be expanded to one hour. But by tradition the half-hour after the national evening news is given over to the hundreds of local affiliate stations around the country to use as they see fit. They have found it a very profitable time to broadcast game shows or half-hour situation comedies, and they are reluctant to give up the income they derive from these programs.

The evening news produced by the three networks is profitable for both the networks and the local stations. The local stations are paid a fee by the network to broadcast the network news, and they profit from this fee since the news—produced by the network—costs them nothing. It is likely that they would also make money from a one-hour newscast, but not as much, they judge, as they do from the game shows and comedies they now schedule.

The result is that the evening news must try to do what cannot reasonably be done: give a decent account of the day's events in twenty-two minutes. What the viewer gets instead is a series of impressions, many of them purely visual, most of them unconnected to each other or to any sense of a history unfolding. Taken together, they suggest a world that is fundamentally ungovernable, where events do not arise out of historical conditions but rather explode from the heavens in a series of disasters that suggest a permanent state of crisis. It is this crisis—highly visual, ahistorical, and unsolvable—which the evening news presents as theater every evening.

The audience for this theater is offered a contradictory pair of responses. On the one hand, it is reassured by the smooth presentation of the news itself, especially the firm voice and steady gaze of the trusty anchorman. Newscasts frequently end with a "human-interest story," often with a sentimental or comic touch. Example: a little girl in Chicago writes Gorbachev a letter, and he answers her, saying that he and President Reagan are trying to work out their differences. This item reassures viewers that all is well, leaders are in command, we can still communicate with each other, and so on. But—and now we come to the other hand—the rest of the broadcast has told a different story. It has shown the audience a world that is out of control and incomprehensible, full of violence, disaster, and suffering. Whatever authority the anchorman may project through his steady manner is undermined by the terror inspired by the news itself.

This is where television news is at its most radical—not in giving publicity to radical causes, but in producing the impression of an ungovernable world. And it produces this impression not because the people who work in television are leftists or anarchists. The anarchy in television news is a direct result of the commercial structure of broadcasting, which introduces into news judgments a single-mindedness more powerful than any ideology: the overwhelming need to keep people watching.

The Educationist as Painkiller

I intended this essay for the consideration of educationists, but wrote it with laymen in mind, or at least those citizens who have wondered why there is so much failure in our schools. Failure of teachers, not students. As is usually the case with me, I conclude that at the heart of significant reform is language education, and the essay adds to what I have said on the matter in "Defending Against the Indefensible." In a somewhat different form, this essay was presented as the keynote address at the annual convention of the Association for Supervision and Curriculum Development, in New Orleans, March 1987.

Of all the popular prejudices nurtured by academics, one of the most enduring is their vigorous contempt for the subject of education and especially for educationists, a word often pronounced with an unmistakable hiss. As I consider myself an educationist, I have had to endure the burden of this prejudice for many years, and, as a consequence, have given some considerable thought to its origins. The prejudice is peculiar, of course, because many of the world's most esteemed philosophers have written extensively on education and may properly be called educationists.

Indeed, Confucius and Plato were what we would call today curriculum specialists. Cicero was less specific in his writing on education than Confucius and Plato, but he too was an educationist if we may take that word to mean a person who is seriously concerned to understand how learning takes place and what part schooling plays in facilitating or obstructing it. In this sense, Quintilian was an educationist, and so were Erasmus, John Locke, Rousseau, and Thomas Jefferson. The great English poet John Milton was so moved by the prospect of writing an essay on education that he called the reforming of education one of "the greatest and noblest designs to be thought on."

In modern times, the list of educationists continues to include formidable intellects—William James, for example, whose *Talks to Teachers* is among the best books on education ever written. Two of the greatest philosophers in this century, Ludwig Wittgenstein and Karl Popper, were elementary-school teachers who of necessity would have thought deeply about educational issues. Wittgenstein's professor at Cambridge, Bertrand Russell, founded a school, and Russell's colleague, Alfred North Whitehead, wrote the impeccable *Aims of Education*. And, of course, America's greatest home-grown systematic philosopher, John Dewey, was an educationist par excellence. In other words, the history of Western philosophy is so bound up with the subject of education that the two can hardly be separated. One might even say that just as it is natural for a physicist upon reaching his deepest understandings to be drawn toward religion, so it is natural for a mature philosopher to turn toward the problems of education.

Why, then, this persistent prejudice against the subject and those who make a profession of its study? Definitive answers await a rich and extensive research project to which sociologists, psychologists, historians, perhaps even anthropologists must contribute their perspectives. I mention anthropology because I suspect the intensity of the prejudice varies from culture to culture. There are places—China, for example—where the prejudice may not exist at all. But if we confine ourselves to the West, we are almost sure to find that it is in the United States that the prejudice is maintained in its most active state. There are great universities in America—Yale, for example—where a student cannot major in the subject. There are even universities where the subject is held in such low esteem that it is possible for a student to major in, of all things, Business Administration but not Education. Of course, Business Administration alumni are usually better positioned to give large gifts to a university than are Education alumni, but this fact by itself cannot explain the pervasiveness of the prejudice. After all, in many universities where the subject of education is considered a side issue, if considered at all, students may major in such subjects as Social Work and Nursing, neither of which promises its graduates the wherewithal to bestow large gifts on Alma Mater. No, I do not think the economics of universities will tell us very much. My own attempts to look into the matter have led in another direction, and by following that path, I believe I have found a way of reversing the prejudice entirely. Even better, I believe my inquiries point toward a solution to a more formidable problem; namely, how to increase our own self-respect.

The usual reason given by standard-brand academics for their distaste for the subject of education is that it is trivial. This they say without much forethought, as if by rote, as if they neither expected nor could resist a rebuttal. When rebuttal comes in the form of a few well-chosen questions of the type "Is it trivial to examine what is meant by learning, and what relation, if any, teaching has to learning?," their attack shifts to a different ground. It is not the triviality of the subject, they say, but the triviality of its professors, many of whom have no deep knowledge of the works of Plato, Cicero, Locke, Rousseau, and other philosophers of similar weight and complexity. This accusation is probably true but is fairly easy to parry, since the same sort of deficiency may be found in professors of other subjects and probably not in smaller measure. Who can deny that there are professors of economics who have not read Ricardo or Marx or even Adam Smith, from beginning to end? Or professors of political science who know little of Machiavelli, let alone Aristotle and Plato? Or professors of psychology who, though Freud considered him his equal, know nothing of the works of Arthur Schnitzler? It is to be doubted that professors of education are as a group more ignorant than professors of other subjects.

The equal distribution of ignorance among a university faculty, however, invites a question whose answer opens the way to a solution that can free us of both the prejudice and some of our own inadequacies. The question is this: Is there anything worse about an ignorant professor of education than an ignorant professor of economics, political science, or psychology? The answer, I believe, is "Yes." All professors are ignorant, but not all ignorances are of equal importance. And there is nothing worse than ignorance on the subject of education. This is so because the subject of education claims dominion over the widest possible territory. It purports to tell us not only what intelligence is but how it may be nurtured; not only what is worthwhile knowledge but how it may be gained; not only what is the good life but how one may prepare for it. There is no other subject—not even philosophy itself—that casts so wide a net, and therefore no other subject that requires of its professors so much genius and wisdom. A professor of political science or economics who lacks insight and brilliance is far from contemptible; indeed, the deficiency may be hardly noticeable. But without brilliance and insight, an educationist is a pitiful sight, bereft, fumbling, nakedly stupid in a way that can never appear as obviously negligent in other subjects. To address the questions posed by Plato, Erasmus, Locke, and Dewey but without their intellectual power, not to mention their spiritual strength, seems arrogant and makes the garden-variety educationist such as myself an object of pity and ridicule.

Those of us—whether schoolteachers, administrators, or professors—who wish to claim the name "educationist" have a problem with what the Greeks called *hubris*. How can we solve it? The solution is simpler than one might suppose. The solution is to diminish the extent of our limitations by diminishing the scope of the subject. In so doing, we may increase not only our stature but also our competence and potency. If I may put it this way: Smaller is better.

Let me take the question of intelligence as my principal example. It is neither seemly nor necessary for educationists to claim to know what intelligence is and how it is nurtured. The claim is grandiose, intelligence too vast and elusive. Educationists like ourselves are not up to the task of understanding the infinite varieties of intelligence, and we fool no one by generating a giant vocabulary that pretends to take hold of the matter. "Where understanding fails," Goethe wrote, "a word will come to take its place." He did not have the vocabulary of educationists in mind, but the aphorism fits. To put it plainly, we know next to nothing about intelligence, in the same sense that medical doctors know next to nothing about health. That is why doctors do not concern themselves with health, and give all their attention to relieving us of sickness. Indeed, their definition of health is the absence of sickness. This is a perfectly sensible way for them to approach matters and accounts in part for the success they have had compared to teachers. By concentrating on the elimination of sickness, doctors give a focus to their objectives and procedures that teachers have not been able to match.

Something quite similar may also be said of lawyers. When have you ever heard of someone consulting a lawyer in order to improve the quality of justice or good citizenship? Whether acting as prosecutors or defenders, lawyers do not trouble themselves about justice or good citizenship—of which, in any case, they know no more than the grocer down the block. They trouble themselves about injustice and bad citizenship, of which they know more than anyone else, and which, it turns out, are much more profitable fields of expertise. Doctors and lawyers, in other words, are painkillers. They are sought out by people who in one way or another have found themselves in trouble and are in need of remedies.

This, then, is the strategy I propose for educationists— that we abandon our vague, seemingly arrogant, and ultimately futile attempts to make children intelligent, and concentrate our attention on helping them avoid being stupid. You may be inclined to think that I am playing with language, proposing a semantic trick. Perhaps. But it is no "mere" semantic trick. By changing the way we talk about our role as teachers, we provide ourselves with necessary constraints and realizable objectives. To return to the medical analogy: The physician knows about sickness and can offer specific advice about how to avoid it. Don't smoke, don't consume too much salt or saturated fat, take two aspirins, take penicillin every four hours, and so forth. I am proposing that the study and practice of education adopt this paradigm precisely. The educationist should become an expert in stupidity and be able to prescribe specific procedures for avoiding it.

I grant that, unlike the study of sickness and injustice, the study of stupidity has rarely been pursued in a systematic way. But this does not mean that the subject has no history. In fact, there are many honorable books that take it as their theme and pursue the matter diligently. My own favorites include the *Analects* of Confucius and the early *Dialogues* of Plato, which are little else but meditations on stupidity. Acknowledging that he did not know what truth is, Socrates spent his time exposing the false beliefs of those who thought they did. I am also partial to Erasmus' *In Praise of Folly*, Jonathan Swift's *Gulliver's Travels*, and, in a more modern vein, Jacques Ellul's *A Critique of the New Commonplaces* and Stephen Jay Gould's *The Mismeasure of Man*. But no matter how many books you read, I believe you will find that there are three conclusions about stupidity that all writers on the subject have reached. These conclusions give educationists a foundation to build on. The first is that everyone practices stupidity, including those who write about it; none of us is ever free of it, and we are most seriously endangered when we think we are safe. That there is an almost infinite supply of stupidity, including our own, should provide educationists with a sense of humility and, incidentally, assurance that they will never become obsolete.

The second conclusion is that stupidity is reducible. At present, educationists consume valuable time in pointless debates over whether or not intelligence is fixed, whether it is mostly genetic or environmental, and even how much of it different races have. Such debates are entirely unnecessary about stupidity. Stupidity is a form of behavior. It is not something we have; it is something we do. Unlike intelligence, it is neither a metaphor nor a hypothetical construct whose presence is inferred by a score on a test. We can see stupidity, and we can hear it. And it is possible to reduce its presence by changing behavior. This should provide educationists with a sense of potency.

The third conclusion is that stupidity is mostly done with the larynx, tongue, lips, and teeth; which is to say, stupidity is chiefly embodied in talk. It is true enough that our ways of talking are controlled by the ways we manage our minds, and no one is quite sure what "mind" is. But we are sure that the main expression of mind is sentences. When we are thinking, we are mostly arranging sentences in our heads. When we are thinking stupidly, we are arranging stupid sentences. Even when we do a nonverbal stupid thing, we have preceded the action by talking to ourselves in such a way as to make us think the act is reasonable. The word, in a word, brings forth the act. This provides educationists with a specific subject matter: the study of those ways of talking that lead to unnecessary mischief, failure, misunderstanding, and pain.

A sense of humility, a sense of potency, a specific subject matter. This is precisely what doctors and lawyers have, and this is what is to be gained if educationists adopt the metaphor of educationist as painkiller. But, of course, this would not be the end of the matter, just the beginning. Two more giant steps are needed to complete the transformation. First, we must construct an anatomy of stupidity, including a thorough taxonomy of it. Just as doctors have identified, named, and described forms of sickness, we must identify, name, and describe forms of stupidity. Then, of course, we must invent two kinds of curricula: one intended for those who teach education to those who will become teachers; subsequently, another for use in schools in various subjects and for children of various ages.

My background does not allow me to presume to say how this might be done. But I want to insist on one point: following the analogy of medical prescription, the curricula must be thought of as strategies for releasing students from the pain of both practicing stupid talk and being victimized by it. Stupidity is like sickness in that some of it we produce ourselves, like ulcers, and some of it is inflicted upon us, like smallpox; our students need protection from both. In this, I fancy that I might make some contribution.

Over the past twenty years, I have made several attempts at constructing an anatomy of stupidity, using as case material, I might add, my own tendencies in that direction. I do not claim to have been entirely successful, but I have been able to isolate thirty-two varieties of stupid talk. These include some of the more obvious forms, such as either-or thinking; overgeneralization; inability to distinguish between facts and inferences; and reification, a disturbingly prevalent tendency to confuse words with things. For the rest of this essay, I should like to give a few additional samples so that you will have a clearer view of what educationists would be experts in remedying, at least as I see it.

I am aware, by the way, that some people do not approve of my using the word "stupidity" as a label for these linguistic practices. Apparently, they feel that the word is too harsh and judgmental to suit the dignity of an educational enterprise. My friend and colleague Henry Perkinson, who has himself tried to construct an anatomy of stupidity, prefers the word "error," as in his wonderful book *The Possibilities of Error*. But I have another friend and colleague, Charles Weingartner, who prefers the word "bullshit," not only because the kind of talk we want to study deserves harsh judgment but also because the word stresses the point that stupidity *is* mostly a kind of talk. I have rejected Professor Weingartner's suggestion, although I will confess that I can think of no more uplifting thought in this matter than to imagine a college catalogue offering courses with such titles as Beginning, Intermediate, and Advanced Bullshit. In any case, here I will use the word "balderdash," as a kind of compromise between Perkinson's gentleness and Weingartner's forthrightness. But whether we call these forms of talk stupidity, errors, mistakes, bullshit, balderdash, or anything else, what they amount to are forms of language behavior that produce unnecessary confusion, pain, and misunderstanding. In some cases, they are conscious tricks people use in order to delude others; in some cases, they are unconscious habits with which we delude ourselves. In either case, someone is victimized.

There are so many varieties of balderdash that I can hope to mention but a few, and to elaborate on even fewer. I will therefore select only those varieties that have some transcendental significance. Now that last sentence is a perfectly good example of balderdash, since I am not certain what "transcendental significance" might mean and neither are you. I needed something to end that sentence with, and since I did not have any clear criteria by which to select my examples, I figured this is the place for some big-time words. Thus we have our first variety of balderdash: pomposity.

Pomposity is the triumph of style over substance, and generally it is not an especially venal form of balderdash. A little pomposity at a graduation ceremony is surely bearable. But it is by no means harmless. Plenty of people are daily victimized by pomposity—made to feel less worthy than they have a right to feel by people who use fancy words, phrases, and sentences to obscure their own insufficiencies. Many people in the teaching business dwell almost exclusively in the realm of pomposity and quite literally would be unable to function if not for the fact that the profession has made this form of balderdash quite respectable.

Generally speaking, pomposity is not a serious affliction among the young, although they are easily victimized by it. There seems to be a correlation between pomposity and aging, as I am beginning to discover myself. Young people, however, suffer badly from a related form of balderdash—what might be called earthiness. Earthiness is based on the assumption that if you use direct, off-color, four-letter words, you somehow are speaking more truth than if you observe the proper language forms. It is the mirror image of pomposity, because, like pomposity, it hopes that people will be so dazzled by the manner of speech that they will not notice the absence of matter. Earthiness becomes dangerous when we convince ourselves that four-letter words are the natural mode of expressing sincerity or honesty or candor.

Another, far more distressing variety of balderdash is called euphemism, and it is exemplified by the word "balderdash" itself. By using the word, I am guilty of euphemizing. But my guilt is not nearly as serious as the guilt of some other, more prominent people. One of the best examples of euphemizing in the past several decades was provided by President Nixon's press secretary, Ronald Ziegler, who instead of using the four-letter word "lies," as in the sentence "The President's previous statements were lies," chose the eleven-letter word "inoperative." President Nixon went Ziegler one better when he chose to say that members of his campaign organization were guilty of an excess of zeal. This was the first time to my knowledge that the word "zeal" has been used as a euphemism for illegal entry, stealing, bribery, and perjury. In any case, euphemism seems to be playing an increasingly important role in American public life. We have had to endure such phrases as "protective reaction strike," "preventive detention," "pacification programs," and one of my all-time favorites, "disinformation." The Reagan administration says it did not lie to the American public about Libya; it merely disseminated disinformation. And on the subject of the present administration, I am obliged to mention one of its more creative euphemisms concerning President Reagan, of whom it is said that he favors a "hands-off managerial style." I assume that the reader understands that this means he doesn't know what the hell is going on.

Euphemism, then, is that form of balderdash wherein we attempt to obscure the nature of reality. Like pomposity, this process is not always harmful, for there are many occasions when simple good taste or good manners require euphemism.

But when euphemism becomes a dominating mode of expression in our institutional life, it is dangerous and ought not to be tolerated. The same is true of euphemism's closest cousin—word magic. Word magic is the process of using language not to obscure reality but to replace it altogether. Word magic is a serious affliction among the young, but they are not the major carriers of the disease. The idea that merely saying something will make it true is the fundamental strategy of America's largest private enterprise—advertising. The advertising industry relies heavily on a population that believes in the magical powers of words to create realities that do not exist. There are many people roaming the streets who appear to believe that the use of Listerine will improve their sex lives or that All-Purpose Tide, if used in abundance, will help solidify their family situation. Actually, if Tide solidifies anything, it is our rivers, not our families, and I am not sure how much more of this balderdash our environment can take.

Word magic is an ancient form of balderdash and is never to be taken lightly. But there is another that is just as ancient and perhaps even more malignant: what some people call fanaticism. There is one type of fanaticism, usually called bigotry, of which I will say nothing—not only because it is so vulgar and obvious but also because teachers are very well aware of it and have made strenuous efforts to help students overcome it. But other forms of fanaticism are not as obvious and therefore may be more dangerous. One of them is what I call Eichmannism, in honor of Adolf Eichmann, who expertly managed to transport about 1 million Jews to the gas chambers but who to the end of his life could see nothing wrong with what he did. Eichmannism is that form of balderdash which accepts as its starting and ending point official definitions, rules, and regulations without regard for the realities of particular situations. The language of Eichmannism is the voice of the organization, which is why it is usually polite, subdued, and even gracious—in a plastic sort of way. A friend of mine actually received a letter once from a mini-Eichmann which began: "We are pleased to inform you that your scholarship for the academic year 1981–1982 has been cancelled." Eichmannism is the cool, orderly, cynical language of the bureaucratic mentality alienated from human interests. It is especially dangerous because it is so utterly detached. That means, among other things, that some of the nicest people turn out to be mini-Eichmanns, and that includes most of us.

Ironically, a version of Eichmannism may be identified in the language of its victims, people so overwhelmed by establishments and systems that they have accepted as unchangeable all the rules and regulations that bureaucrats administer. This acceptance frequently takes the form of deifying "they" and "them," as in "They won't let me do this," or, "There is no way of dealing with them." The fact is that every system, no matter how impersonal, is in the end controlled by people and is therefore susceptible to modification. There is, of course, no great harm in using a word like "establishment" as long as it is understood that the term is merely a metaphor for organized power. But to the extent that terms like "the establishment" and "the power structure" are assumed to mean a non-human agent that perpetually frustrates individual human enterprise, then they are the equivalent of saying, "The Devil made me do it." It is the greatest achievement of Eichmannism that in the end the language of the oppressor and the language of the oppressed are identical. They both end up saying, "I can't help what I am doing."

Two other varieties of balderdash require a word or two of explanation here, and one of them is what is usually called superstition. Superstition is ignorance presented under the cloak of authority. A superstition is a belief, usually expressed in definitive terms, for which there is no verifiable, factual basis; for instance, that the country in which you live is a finer place, all things considered, than all other countries. Or that the religion into which you were born confers upon you some special standing with the cosmos that is denied to other people. The teaching profession, it grieves me to say, has generated dozens of similar superstitions—for example, the belief that people with college degrees are educated, or the belief that students who are given lessons in grammar will improve their writing, or that one's knowledge of anything can be objectively measured. For me, the most perilous of all these superstitions is the belief, expressed in a variety of ways, that the study of literature and other humanistic subjects will result in one's becoming a more decent, liberal, tolerant, and civilized human being. Whenever someone alludes to this balderdash in my presence, I try to remind myself that during the last two decades men with Ph.D.s in the humanities and social sciences, many of them working for the Pentagon, have been responsible for killing more people in any given week than the Mafia has managed since its inception.

Finally, I want to mention an exceedingly depressing form of balderdash that never seems to diminish in popularity, namely, sloganeering. Sloganeering consists largely of ritualistic utterances intended to communicate solidarity. The utterances themselves may have meanings quite contrary to those the sloganeers intend—as in the mercifully obsolete expression "Power to the People." Very few sloganeers who used this expression could possibly have wanted the people to have all that power since, were it possible, most of the people probably would have put an immediate end to campus dissent, women's liberation, black activism, and other troublesome political movements. What "Power to the People" really meant, of course, was "Power to Our People," a perfectly legitimate sentiment provided you have made clear to yourself and others that that is what you are saying. The major problem with sloganeering, whether shouted from a picket line or convention hall, or displayed on a car bumper, is that it is a substitute for thought, indeed a repudiation of thought. The young are afflicted badly with this sort of balderdash, of course, and if we could get them to restrict its use to cheering at football games, we would be making some progress. But as long as slogans are used to simulate ideas, no matter in whose name, we have a serious problem in need of treatment.

Now, I know that the ways in which I have stated these forms of stupidity are inadequate. Nor do I claim that these are necessarily the most crippling habits of mind that afflict us. Even if some of them were, I assure you that I have no special expertise in imagining how we could get ourselves and our students to avoid them. I mean them to be taken only as examples of the behaviors we might identify as the focus of our activities as educationists.

Education as the art of healing the mind is in its infancy. In saying this, I intend no disrespect to the great educationists of the past. For at least 2,500 years, there were men called doctors of medicine, many of them brilliant and some of them useful. And yet, prior to this century, the whole history of medicine was simply the history of the placebo effect. Doctors have become effective, systematic healers only within the recent memory of living people. Perhaps in fifty years we shall be able to say the same of educationists.

Etiquette

This and the next piece need little advance comment, except to say that the second one is written in the only form (so it seems to me) in which it is now possible to speak of nuclear war. The language of everyday political commentary is incapable of expressing what is at stake. One must therefore speak about how we speak about the subject.

It is no secret that human beings have been replaced by baskets at toll-booth stations throughout the country. I, for one, am not at all sentimental about the substitution since in the first place, human money-collecting on highways is undignified and probably boring, and in the second place, baskets are much better suited to the job than human hands. Baskets are bigger and never clammy. A basket cannot make change, but that is only a temporary deficiency. With very little effort, baskets can be programmed to subtract 25 cents from anything up to a thousand-dollar bill. There would then remain only one problem for the basket. It cannot answer such questions as "What exit do I take if I'm going to New Hyde Park?" or, "How far is it to the next rest station?" Theoretically, a basket can be programmed to answer these and any other reasonable questions, although it is unlikely, even in theory, that a basket could ever respond intelligently to such a remark as "The baby just threw up. Do you have a towel or something?" Nevertheless, that problem can be solved by keeping one human being, supplied abundantly with towels, in some sort of emergency booth.

This solves all of the problems from the basket's point of view. But there still remain several for the motorists, almost all of which concern their sensibilities. Each basket has an appendage that has been programmed to flash "Thank you" after the motorist has performed her civic duty. Common courtesy, of course, compels the motorist to respond. In these circumstances, however, one feels quite silly saying "You're welcome," unless one has some sort of assurance that one's courtesy has been understood and perhaps appreciated. I know many motorists who refuse to say anything to the basket *only* because they assume the basket is indifferent to their responses. This is perfectly understandable, but it could be corrected if the basket were programmed to respond to a human's "You're welcome" by flashing something like "Well, it *was* awfully nice of you."

There still remains the problem of what one is to do or say when the coin has missed the basket. After you've retrieved the coin and thrown it in, the basket's appendage still says "Thank you," but unquestionably the remark now has a sarcastic ring, which only adds to one's sheepishness. In such cases, the sensitive motorist will invariably say something like "I'm terribly sorry," to which the appendage could not, in all courtesy, reply, "Well it *was* awfully nice of you." That simply would not do. Perhaps the basket can be programmed to reply, "That's quite all right. Others frequently make the same mistake."

Such a reply would make the motorist feel that her efforts are appreciated, and she could proceed down the highway with that exhilarated air that comes to those who have exchanged cordialities with somebody, or something.

Megatons for Anthromegs

Now that we know how much our children's dreams are plagued by fears of a nuclear holocaust, it is time we adults did something about it. Since it would be immature, not to mention irresponsible, to actually eliminate nuclear weapons, what is needed is a new vocabulary of nuclear war, a vocabulary uncluttered by the associations which generate fear and trembling.

This I have begun to do. I hope my lexicon, when completed, will form the basis of a rhetoric of reassurance that will pacify our children's dreams and help the rest of us contemplate with courage and dignity the realities of nuclear war.

Below, I have placed currently used terms on the left. To the right of each is the term I offer in its place. I have also included some small elaboration of the superiority of my term over the one it would replace.

ONE MILLION PEOPLE   ANTHROMEG

It is disconcerting and unnecessarily emotional to talk of millions of people, especially if they are going to die. What could be more objective and detached, and at the same time more calming, than the statement, "Ten megatons kills twenty anthromegs"? Ask any man if he is willing to lose, say, 65 anthromegs if he could thereby defeat the Russians, and he will immediately say "Yes." If you ask him if he is willing to lose 65 million people, he will become confused and depressed.

NUCLEAR ATTACK   AERIAL VISITATION

If the Russians attack us, they will not come with ice pellets. "Attack" *means* "nuclear attack." Why provide ourselves with a double reminder, especially one so anxiety-producing? "Aerial visitation" will help to eliminate unreasonable fears about the future and will do more to encourage us to plan ahead with enthusiasm. Who could possibly get upset by a sign which says: "In Case of Aerial Visitation, Drive over Bridge"? Tell a man that in the event of an aerial visitation his child will be kept at school, and he will probably ask, "And when may I come to get him?"

KILLING BY NUCLEAR WEAPONS   THERMALICIDE

Men have invented an illustrious list of technical words to describe with precision and detachment the various types of killing. "Thermalicide" extends the list by one by providing us with an unemotional, scientific denotation of a perfectly natural, albeit unpleasant, human activity. Besides, there are far too many disgusting associations attached to "genocide."

DEATH BY NUCLEAR WEAPONS   CULMINATING EXPERIENCE

"To culminate" means to reach one's highest point, a virtual certainty when one has been exploded by a nuclear weapon. "To experience" means to undergo actively, another certainty when within range of a nuclear explosion. "Culminating experience" is, therefore, a perfectly precise description of the process.

RADIATION   FILTERATION

Who would not prefer being filterated as against radiated, even if the effect is the same? One filters cigarette smoke or swimming pools or lubricating oil. The word forcefully suggests that the result of the process is some sort of purity, a most apt connotation. For, after all, is it not purifying to suffer?

FALLOUT SHELTER   PROTECTIVE RESIDENCE

Although not much has been said about it lately, when the subject of fallout shelters comes up there is usually a considerable amount of hysteria. It is to be expected. What man would desire to live in a "shelter" even for a day? The word is ominous. It hints at alienation and ultimate isolation. "Protective residence" is another matter. The term suggests an extension of one's home—comfy, warm, intimate, familiar. Moreover, the moral question of whether or not you are obligated to allow others entrance is easily settled. A "shelter" connotes public domain, but a man's "residence" is his castle. That's that.

SURVIVORS   THE UNCULMINATED

Is there a more desperate-sounding word in our language than "survivors"? It conjures up visions of groping, disoriented people and surrounding chaos. "The unculminated" logically follows from "culminating experience" and at the same time suggests unfulfilled ambitions, unsatisfied desires; in short, the continuation of life.

The vocabulary presented above is, of course, only a beginning—basic talk, as it were. In order to suggest how such a vocabulary might be used to create a new rhetoric of re-assurance, I have composed below a short paragraph which describes in inoffensive language the realities of thermo-nuclear war:

American scientists assure us that our capacity for ther-malicide is the greatest in the world. This fact will, of course, deter our enemies from attempting it on us. But should our enemies decide to make aerial visitations, we will persevere. If every family has provided itself with a protective residence, the extent of filteration will be sharply minimized. And even if our enemies should launch a 300-megaton aerial visitation, probably no more than 50 or 60 anthromegs will have a culminating experience. Those who are unculminated may remain in their protective residences until all danger of ther-malicide is past.

Sleep in peace, my children.

The Conservative Outlook

Every age has its own special forms of imperialism. And so does each conqueror. In the eighteenth and nineteenth centuries, when the British mastered the art, their method of invasion was to send their navy, then their army, then their administrators, and finally their educational system. The Americans now do it differently. We send our television shows. The method has much to recommend it. Neither armies nor navies clash by night; the invasion occurs without loss of life and without much resistance. It is also both pleasurable and quick. In a few years, we shall be able to boast that the sun never sets on an American television show. The Russians have not yet figured out what is happening. When Khrushchev said of the West (but mostly thinking of America), "We will bury you," he spoke as a pre-electronic man, thinking in terms of nineteenth-century Realpolitik. Had he been a more careful student of Marx, he would have remembered that political consciousness is borne on the wings of technology. He might then have grasped that electromagnetic waves penetrate more deeply than armies. Perhaps Gorbachev understands. But if the Russians keep relying on nineteenth-century forms of imperialism while continuing to make terrible television shows, they may find themselves turning into a Third World country.

One would think, of course, that Europeans would be fully aware of what is happening. And many are. Those who are not are probably confounded by the fact that the American method of imperialism is more subtle than it might seem. I said that what we do is send our television programs. Not exactly. What we really send is our idea of television. To understand what is meant by the idea of television, one must allow a distinction between a technology and a medium. A technology is to a medium what the brain is to the mind. Like the brain, a technology is a physical apparatus. Like the mind, a medium is a use to which a physical apparatus is put. Television is essentially the same technology in America and in Europe. But for forty years, it has been two different media, used in different ways, for different purposes, based on different suppositions.

Each of the next two essays bears on this point and the issues that arise from it. The first is a lecture given in Austria to The Club of Vienna, a group of conservative business people and academics.

As a visitor in your country—indeed, as one who does not even know your language well enough to use it in these circumstances—I feel obliged to add something to the introduction I have been given. You are entitled to know at the start from what cultural and political perspectives I see the world, since everything I will have to say here reflects a point of view quite likely different from your own. I am what may be called a conservative. This word, of course, is ambiguous, and you may have a different meaning for it from my own. Perhaps it will help us to understand each other if I say that from my point of view, Ronald Reagan is a radical. It is true enough that he continually speaks of the importance of preserving such traditional institutions and beliefs as the family, childhood, the work ethic, self-denial, and religious piety. But in fact President Reagan does not care one way or another whether any of this is preserved. I do not say that he is *against* preserving tradition; I say only that this is not where his interests lie. You cannot have failed to notice that he is mostly concerned to preserve a free-market economy, to encourage the development of what is new, and to keep America technologically progressive. He is what may be called a free-market extremist. All of which is to say he is devoted to capitalism. A capitalist cannot afford the pleasures of conservatism, and of necessity regards tradition as an obstacle to be overcome. How the idea originated that capitalists are conservative is something of a mystery to me. Perhaps it is explained by nothing more sinister than that capitalists are inclined to wear dark suits and matching ties.

In any case, it is fairly easy to document that capitalists have been a force for radical social change since the eighteenth century, especially in the United States. This is a fact that Alexis de Tocqueville noticed when he studied American institutions in the early nineteenth century. "The American lives," he wrote, "in a land of wonders; everything around him is in constant movement, and every movement seems an advance. Consequently, in his mind the idea of newness is closely linked with that of improvement. Nowhere does he see any limit placed by nature to human endeavor; in his eyes something that does not exist is just something that has not been tried."

This is the credo of capitalists the world over, and, I might add, is the source of much of the energy and ingenuity that have characterized American culture for almost two hundred years. No people have been more entranced by newness—and particularly technological newness—than Americans.

That is why our most important radicals have always been capitalists, especially capitalists who have exploited the possibilities of new technologies. The names that come to mind are Samuel Morse, Alexander Graham Bell, Thomas Edison, Henry Ford, William Randolph Hearst, Samuel Goldwyn, Henry Luce, Alan Dumont, and Walt Disney, among many others. These capitalist-radicals, inflamed by their fascination for new technologies, created the twentieth century. If you are happy about the twentieth century, you have them to thank for it.

But as we all know, in every virtue there lurks a contrapuntal vice. I believe Tocqueville had this in mind in the passage I quoted. He meant to praise our ambition and vitality but at the same time to condemn our naïveté and rashness. He meant, in particular, to say that a culture that exalts the new for its own sake, that encourages the radical inclination to exploit what is new and is therefore indifferent to the destruction of the old, that such a culture runs a serious risk of becoming trivial and dangerous, especially dangerous to itself.

This is exactly what is happening in the United States in the latter part of the twentieth century. In today's America, the idea of newness not only is linked to the idea of improvement but is the definition of improvement. If anyone should raise the question, What improves the human spirit?, or even the more mundane question, What improves the quality of life?, Americans are apt to offer a simple formulation: That which is new is better, that which is newest is best.

The cure for such a stupid philosophy is conservatism. My version, not President Reagan's. A true conservative, like myself, knows that technology always fosters radical social change. A true conservative also knows that it is useless to pretend that technology will not have its way with a culture. But a conservative recognizes a difference between rape and seduction. The rapist cares nothing for his victim. The seducer must accommodate himself to the will and temperament of the object of his desires. Indeed, he does not want a victim so much as an accomplice. What I am saying is that technology can rape a culture or be forced to seduce it. The aim of a genuine conservative in a technological age is to control the fury of technology, to make it behave itself, to insist that it accommodate itself to the will and temperament of a people. It is his best hope that through his efforts a modicum of charm may accompany the union of technology and culture.

The United States is the most radical society in the world. It is in the process of conducting a vast, uncontrolled social experiment which poses the question, Can a society preserve any of its traditional virtues by submitting all of its institutions to the sovereignty of technology? Those of us who live in America and who are inclined to say "No" are therefore well placed to offer warnings to our European cousins—who are themselves wondering whether or not to participate fully in such an experiment.

In order to give focus to my advice, I shall confine myself to the technology of television, which, at the moment, poses the most serious threat to traditional patterns of life in all industrialized nations, including your own. And I hope you will forgive me if I begin by quoting Karl Marx. Marx once wrote, "There is a specter haunting Europe." The specter he had in mind was the rising up of the proletariat. The specter *I* have in mind is commercial television. Everywhere one looks in Europe—West Germany, Sweden, France, Holland, Switzerland, Denmark—the ghostly form of commercial television is making its presence felt. That it threatens the foundations of each West European nation ought to be obvious, but, one fears, the possibility has not been sufficiently discussed.

In Paris alone there are seven advertiser-supported television stations, and now an eighth one has been installed in three Paris subway stations. It consists of 150 closed-circuit units, each unit carrying thirty minutes of programming: four minutes of news about the subway system, sixteen minutes' worth of programs, and ten minutes of advertising. The ads cost $7,500 per week for each thirty-second spot. In the understatement of the year, the marketing director of the Paris subway system said, "It's a way of changing the ambience of the subway station." Of course, this man has confused cause and effect. If the French require television entertainment when they go from one end of town to the other, then we may say that it is not the ambience of the subway that has changed but the ambience of French culture. We may take "ambience" to mean, here, the psychic habits of the people.

In England, which has two commercial television stations, extended political commercials have already appeared. In one such commercial, a star of "Monty Python's Flying Circus," John Cleese, did a fifteen-minute comedy routine, the purpose of which was to solicit support for a new political party. British advertising agencies believe this mixing of comedy and politics is the wave of the future. You get support for a party by having a party.

In Denmark, which has consistently opposed commercial television, plans have now been completed to allow advertising on the second national television channel, which begins broadcasting in 1988. As is presently the case in Austria, advertising for tobacco and alcohol will be prohibited. Also banned are ads for medicine, banks, political parties, and religious organizations, as well as commercials aimed specifically at young people. The Danes are usually a realistic and clear-headed people. But does anyone believe that the specter of commercial television will be appeased by such compromises? Perhaps. And perhaps it will be appeased in Austria as well. But if it is not, you can lose very quickly much that you love and admire about your country. What I should like to do, then, is to frighten you by making a series of prophecies about what will occur if Austria allows its television technology to become a free-market commodity. These prophecies are largely based on the experiences of my country, which is the only nation, at present, where commercial interests dominate television.

By way of preface, I want to make two points. The first is that in principle, a conservative is not obliged to be opposed to state-controlled broadcasting. One of the best-known American conservatives of this century, Herbert Hoover, our thirty-first President, was appalled at the prospect of opening up broadcasting to commercial interests. In 1923, when he was Secretary of Commerce, he expressed in the most emphatic terms his hope that radio, which he viewed as an instrument of public education, would be kept free of the marketplace. There can be no doubting that were he to see American television today, he would deplore the fact that his advice was ignored. While conservatives are rightly suspicious of state authority and therefore of state-controlled television, they need not be so foolish as to suppose that the state is the only antagonist of freedom of choice, or necessarily the worst.

Which leads me to my second point. If one asks the question, Does a state-controlled television system limit freedom of expression and choice?, the answer is, obviously, Yes, it does. But it is extremely naive to believe that a free-market television system does not also limit freedom. In the United States, where television is controlled by advertising revenues, its principal function is, naturally enough, to deliver audiences to advertisers. The more popular a program is, the more money it can charge an advertiser for commercials. Last year, when the Bill Cosby Show got under way, the cost for thirty seconds of advertising time on that program was $50,000. This year, when the Cosby Show is number one in the ratings, the cost is $300,000 for thirty seconds. What is popular pays and therefore stays; what is in arrears disappears. American television limits freedom of expression and choice because its only criterion of merit and significance is popularity. And this, in turn, means that almost anything that is difficult or serious or goes against the grain of popular prejudices will not be seen.

What will happen if commercial television takes hold in a serious way in Austria? By serious commercial television, I mean a system that is largely supported by advertising revenues, and that has a minimum of government regulations about what can be broadcast and when. Should anything like this come to Austria, here's what I predict:

First, commercial television will increase pressure to extend the number of hours of television broadcasting each day. There is simply too much money at stake to allow any part of the day to go unused. Where there is one fully functioning commercial channel, there will be pressure for others to emerge. When there are two or more, the channels will compete with each other for the audience's attention, and for advertising money. This will lead to an increase in American-style television programs—fast-paced, visually dynamic programs with an emphasis on interesting images rather than serious content. This means an increase in comedy, car chases, violence, and sexually oriented material.

To hold their audiences, state-controlled channels will be forced to compete with commercial-style programming, and will also become similar to American television. This is exactly what has happened to the BBC in England and the Public Broadcasting System in America.

As audiences come to expect fast-paced, visually exciting programs, they will begin to find issue-oriented public-affairs and news programs dull. To compete with entertainment programs, news and public-affairs programs will become more visual and more personality-oriented. As a result, there will be a decline in the public's capacity to understand and discuss events and issues in a serious way.

Of course, television advertising will draw advertisers away from newspapers and magazines. Some newspapers and magazines will go out of business; others will change their format and style to compete with television for audiences, and to match the style of thought promoted by television. They will become more picture-oriented and will feature dramatic headlines, celebrities, and sensational stories. Of course, there will be less substantive and complex writing. For some idea of what I mean, I suggest you look at America's newest, most successful national newspaper, *USA Today;* you ought also to take note of the fact that one of America's oldest and most distinguished literary magazines, *Harper's,* has found it necessary to reduce substantially the length of its articles and stories in order to accommodate the reduced attention span of its readers.

The uses of books will also change. I suspect there will be an erosion of the concept of the common reader, the type of person who gets most of his or her literary experience and information from novels and general non-fiction books. There will almost certainly be an increase in both illiteracy and aliteracy (an aliterate being a person who can read but doesn't). It has been estimated that in the United States there are now 60 million illiterates, and according to a report from our Librarian of Congress, there may be an equal number of aliterates. In any case, a general impatience with books will develop, especially with books in which language is used with subtlety to express complex ideas. Most likely there will be a decline in readers' analytical and critical skills. According to the results of standardized tests given in schools, this has been happening in the United States for the past twenty-five years. I suspect concern for history will also decline, to be replaced by a consuming interest in the present.

The effect on political life will be devastating. There will be less emphasis on issues, substance, and ideology, an increase in the importance of image and style. Politicians will have greater concern for moment-to-moment shifts in public opinion, less concern for long-range policies. Unless the use of television for political campaigns is strictly prohibited, elections may be decided by which party spends more on television and media consultants. Even if political commercials are prohibited, politicians will appear on entertainment programs and will almost certainly be asked to give testimonials for non-political products such as cars, beer, and breakfast foods. The line between political life and entertainment will blur, and movie stars may be taken seriously as political candidates.

Once the population becomes accustomed to spending much of its time watching television—in the United States, the average household has television on about eight hours a day—there will be a decrease in activities outside the home: fewer and smaller gatherings in parks, beer halls, concert halls, and other public places. As street life decreases, there may well be an increase in street crime.

Young people will, of course, become disaffected from school and reading. Children's games are likely to disappear. In fact, it will become important to keep children watching television because they will be a major consumer group. In the United States, children watch 5,000 hours of television before they enter kindergarten and 16,000 hours by high school's end. Commercial television does not dislike children; it simply cannot afford the idea of childhood. Consumerhood takes precedence.

Naturally, family life will be significantly changed. There will be less interaction among family members, certainly less talk between parents and children. Such talk as there is will be noticeably different from what you are now accustomed to. The young will speak of matters that once were confined to adults. Commercial television is a medium that does not segregate its audience, and therefore all segments of the population share the same symbolic world. You may find that in the end the line between adulthood and childhood has been erased entirely.

Since Austria already has some television commercials, you have seen how commercials stress the values of youth, how they stress consumption, the immediate gratification of desires, the love of the new, a contempt for what is old. Television screens saturated with commercials promote the Utopian and childish idea that all problems have fast, simple, and technological solutions. You must banish from your mind the naive but commonplace notion that commercials are about products. They are about products in the same sense that the story of Jonah is about the anatomy of whales. Which is to say, they aren't. They are about values and myths and fantasies. One might even say they form a body of religious literature, a montage of voluminous, visualized sacred texts that provide people with images and stories around which to organize their lives. To give you some idea of exactly how voluminous, I should tell you that the average American will have seen approximately 1 million television commercials, at the rate of a thousand per week, by the age of twenty. By the age of sixty-five, the average American will have seen more than 2 million television commercials. Commercial television adds to the Decalogue several impious commandments, among them that thou shalt have no other gods than consumption, thou shalt despise what is old, thou shalt seek to amuse thyself continuously, and thou shalt avoid complexity like the ten plagues that afflicted Egypt.

Perhaps you are thinking that I exaggerate the social and psychic results of the commercialization of television and that, in any case, what has happened in the United States could not happen in Austria. If you are, you overestimate the power of tradition and underestimate the power of technology. To enliven your sense of the forces unleashed by technological change, you need only remind yourself of what the automobile has brought to Austria. Has it not changed the nature of your cities, created the suburbs, poisoned your air and forests, restructured your economy? You must not mislead yourselves by what you know about Austrian culture as of 1987. Austria is still living in the age of Gutenberg. Commercial television attacks such backwardness with astonishing ferocity. For example, at the present time, less than 20 percent of the Austrian population watches television in the evening. A commercial television system will find this situation intolerable. In the United States, about 75 percent of the adult population watches television during evening hours, and broadcasters find even those numbers unsatisfactory. In Austria, such commercials as you have are bunched together so that they do not interfere with the continuity of programs. Such a situation makes no sense in a commercial system. The whole idea is precisely to interrupt the continuity of programs so that one's thoughts cannot stray too far from considerations of consumership. Indeed, the aim is to obliterate the distinction between a program and a commercial. In Austria, you do not have many advertising agencies, and those you have are small and without great influence. In America, our advertising agencies are among the largest and most powerful corporations in the world. The merger of Doyle, Dane, Bernbach with BBD&O and Needham Harper will provide the new company with the possibility of $5.5 billion in billings each year, and possibly $500 million per year for American network television alone. This is serious money and these are serious radicals. They cannot afford to permit a culture to retain old ideas about work or religion or politics or childhood. And it will not be long before they and their kind show up in Austria.

If, like me, you claim allegiance to an authentic conservative philosophy, one that seeks to preserve that which nourishes the spirit, you would be wise to approach all proposals for a free-market television system with extreme caution. Indeed, I will go further than that: it is either hypocrisy or ignorance to argue that the transformation of Austria or any other country from a print-based culture to a television-based culture can leave that country's traditions intact. Conservatives know this is nonsense, and so they worry. Radicals also know this is nonsense. But they don't care.

Remembering the Golden Age

This essay originated as a talk given in Stockholm to a group of Swedish television writers and producers who were gathered to consider how television might be improved in Sweden. On that occasion, I was specifically asked to avoid being negative, and to address the question, How can television be used to create a true theater for the masses?

During the past several years, I have spent a good deal of my time blaming television for many of the more obvious dysfunctions from which Western culture—and especially America—is now suffering. It has been pointed out to me that I do this because I am by nature a negative person, always ready to condemn what is wrong rather than to praise what is right. Several of my students have even gone so far as to observe that had I lived during the period of incunabula—during the first fifty years of the printing press—I would have burdened everyone with a long list of depressing prophecies about the dangers of the machine-made book and universal literacy. But my students are only half right. Assuming I had the brains to see what was happening in the year 1500, I would certainly have warned the Holy See that the printing press would place the word of God on every Christian's kitchen table, and, as a consequence, the authority of the Church hierarchy would be put in jeopardy. Had I been granted a papal audience, I would have warned the Pope that armed with a printing press, Martin Luther was more than a malcontent priest suffering from a bad case of constipation. The printed word made him a serious revolutionary.

I might also have warned the local princes that their days were numbered, that printing would give form to a new idea of nationhood which would make local potentates obsolete. And if the Brotherhood of Alchemists had allowed me to give the keynote address at their annual convention, I would have told them to go into another line of work, that printing would give great impetus to inductive science and that alchemy would not stand against the glare of publicly shared scientific knowledge. I would also have told any wandering bards who came my way that within a hundred years their trade would lie in ruins, that tribal lays and epic poetry were doomed, and that they would be wise to urge their trainees to turn their talents to writing essays and novels.

Now, not every one of these prophecies foretells a bad thing. That is why I said my students are only half right. Whether or not a prophecy is negative depends on your point of view. For example, since most of you are Lutherans, you probably would have cheered the breakup of the Holy Roman Empire. The Catholics of those times would, of course, have mourned its passing. As a Jew, I wouldn't have given a damn one way or the other: it makes little difference whether a pogrom is inspired by Martin Luther or Pope Leo X. In any case, the point I want to make is that the changes brought about by new media benefit some, harm others, and to a few don't make much of a difference. This is as true of television as it was of the printing press or any other important medium, although in the case of television there are very few indeed who are not affected in one way or another. For most of you here, television will provide a gratifying career. On the other hand, and in the long run, television may bring an end to the careers of schoolteachers, since school itself was an invention of the printing press and must stand or fall on the issue of how much importance the printed word will have in the future. As Harold Innis liked to put it, new media break up old knowledge monopolies; indeed, create new conceptions of knowledge, even new conceptions of politics. Ronald Reagan, for example, would not be President of the United States were it not for television, which is good for him and the interests he represents, but not so good for the poor and vulnerable.

But I am not here to speak of television's harmful consequences; indeed, I have been forbidden to do so. I have been reduced to the indignity of positive thinking, which leaves me no alternative other than to talk about how television might benefit the Swedish people; specifically, about how you might use television to create a true theater of the masses. When I am finished, I hope you will tell people that I am not by nature a negative person.

My muted optimism in this matter is rooted in the fact that a true television theater of the masses once actually existed in America. I should like to tell you about it because the conditions that produced it exist today in Sweden. The conditions that ruined it also exist in Sweden, but I am not permitted to discuss that. What follows, then, is a bit of American television history, some of which might astonish you. For example, between the years 1948 and 1958, approximately 1,500 fifty-two-minute plays were performed "live" on American television. (For the benefit of the young ones present, I should explain that the term "live" means that these plays were performed at the precise moment they were seen by the television audience, a condition which since the advent of videotape and the widespread use of film has become increasingly rare; "fifty-two minutes" describes the actual running time of the play, eight minutes of the hour being subtracted for commercial messages, the listing of credits, and publicity for the next week's play.)

There is no doubt that American television's finest dramatic moments were provided by these fifty-two-minute hours, particularly by such weekly series as the Kraft Television Theater (1947–58), the Philco-Goodyear Playhouse (1948–50), and Studio One (1948–57). These programs began by presenting adaptations of classic and established contemporary novels but by 1950 had shifted to original dramatic work. By that time, such producers and directors as Worthington Miner, Fred Coe, Delbert Mann, Arthur Penn, and John Frankenheimer had assembled about them several gifted young writers who were prepared to devote their collective talents to a serious exploration of television's artistic resources. Included in that group, among others, were Reginald Rose, Tad Mosel, Robert Alan Aurthur, Horton Foote, Rod Serling, J. P. Miller, and Gore Vidal. None, however, wrote more fittingly for television than Paddy Chayefsky, whose name, along with Edward R. Murrow's, symbolizes what romantics call "the golden age of television."

Chayefsky was to the "original" television drama what Ibsen was to the "social drama," which is to say that he was one of its first creators and certainly its most distinguished one. Like Ibsen, he achieved an almost perfect union of form and content. Critics have observed, for example, that the effects that Ibsen achieved in *A Doll's House* and *Ghosts* were a function not only of his themes, with which audiences were certainly familiar in 1879 and 1881, but also of the stark, simple, and economical form in which he stated them. Social dramas had been written before Ibsen, but it remained for him to discover the proper form for dramatizing social problems.

Chayefsky, of course, did not write for the stage behind a proscenium arch, viewed from a distance in a darkened theater. He wrote for a seventeen-inch screen situated in a family living room, on which the only colors were varying shades of gray. He also had to present his story, from start to finish, in fifty-two minutes, and he could make two assumptions with absolute assurance: that his play would be interrupted at least twice for commercial messages, and that he would have to attract his audience instantly or lose much of it to other channels. He knew, too, as did his director, Delbert Mann, that the picture on the television screen is considerably cruder in visual definition than that on a motion-picture screen. So Chayefsky wrote his plays in anticipation of the audience's observing the players in almost unrelenting "close-up."

Chayefsky realized that some of these technical-aesthetic conditions could create, as could perhaps no other medium, a sense of utter and absolute reality; could create the illusion that what the audience was seeing was not a mere play but life as seen through a seventeen-inch, nearly square hole. Beginning with a play called *Holiday Song,* which dealt with a rabbi's re-examination of his faith in God, Chayefsky created a series of dramas that have often been characterized as "small" masterpieces, sometimes referred to as "kitchen" dramas, since much of the action seemed to take place in family kitchens. In any case, they were plays about unexceptional people who existed for fifty-two minutes in wholly unexceptional situations. The plots were uncluttered, undaring, and highly compressed. They had few unexpected turns, little action, no treachery, no perversion, and no heroic gestures (in the traditional sense). Chayefsky's stories were "small" very much as Sherwood Anderson's stories are small.

The setting was New York, not small-town Ohio, but like Anderson, Chayefsky explored in economical but meticulous detail the agonizing problems of small people. And thus he elevated the status of both the problems and the people who suffered them. In fact, Chayefsky once remarked that "Your mother, sister, brothers, cousins, friends—all of these are better subjects for drama than Iago." He was talking, of course, about television drama.

Chayefsky's most widely known play, *Marty,* tells the story of an unmarried, inarticulate butcher who is attracted to a sensitive but homely woman. Marty's friends attempt to dissuade him from seeing the woman because she is, in their words, "a dog." His mother, who fears being abandoned, resents the woman bitterly. Against a backdrop of such universal themes as man's need of loving and being loved, his fear of living alone, and his need to communicate, Chayefsky pursued his "small" story with persistent literalness, concluding with an equally "small" crisis in which Marty decides, against the protests of his friends and family, to phone the woman and ask her for a date. On the stage or in a novel, the plot would be too flimsy to carry much dramatic weight. When the play was adapted for the movies, it required more "movement" or action and the addition of at least one subplot. On the television screen, however, the play was an artistic triumph, producing a disturbing and edifying illusion of intimacy. Perhaps no other medium is better suited to the "slice of life" drama than television, a fact that is apparently well known to Ingmar Bergman.

Chayefsky was not alone in exploring the unique qualities of the television screen, but other writers did not place the same emphasis on the explication, in naturalistic terms, of the problems of ordinary people. Reginald Rose, for example, favored the "message" play, such as *Twelve Angry Men* and *Tragedy in a Temporary Town,* in which he laid bare some of the more contemptible prejudices of his audience. Gore Vidal wrote television's most literate satire, *Visit to a Small Planet,* which in simulated Shavian style condemned man's most persistent talent, the making of war. Rod Serling examined the motivations and pressures of "big business" in his highly successful *Patterns.* And Alvin Sapinsley experimented with poetic dramas, one of which, *Lee at Gettysburg,* was suggestive in its rhythm and compression of the poetic dramas of radio.

Whatever differences existed among these writers, the success of each may be attributed to his ability to recognize certain inescapable facts about the medium, its audience, and the environment in which the audience characteristically viewed the play. For example, television drama seems to be singularly effective when focused on people rather than plots, places, or even ideas. As mentioned before, the "normal" view of the players on a television screen is the close-up. As a consequence, the human face is given such a continued and forceful presence that it tends to become the overriding emphasis of the play, whether the author intends it or not. Bridges falling down and planes zooming high may be thrillingly pictured in films or described in novels. But on live television, of course, the space limitations in a studio make them impossible. Even in televised film sequences, such actions are not dramatically persuasive because of the smallness of the screen and the relatively crude definition of the image. Television, as one director put it, is a "psychoanalytic medium." What television drama does best is to show faces and to suggest what is behind them. Rod Serling once wrote, "The key to TV drama is intimacy, and the facial study on a small screen carries with it a meaning and a power far beyond its usage in the motion picture."

As these writers and directors discovered, television drama is also at its best when highly compressed. There is little time for subplots or for much elaboration of the main plot. The television dramatist, like the short story writer, has time only to relate a bare narrative and evoke a mood, which he does with the help of the camera. Occasionally, the writer is faced with the problem of expanding a brief story, but typically his problem is the reverse. "Television," Chayefsky wrote, "cannot take a thick, fully woven fabric of drama. It can only handle simple lines of movement and consequently smaller moments of crisis."

We must remember also that television is family entertainment viewed within the home. In an earlier time, producers and writers believed that this imposed limitations on both the language and the themes of television plays. Nymphomania, homosexuality, or incest might be maturely explored in the theater or in other literary forms, but (they believed) on television such subjects tended to be shocking, not only because of television's unselected audience but especially because of the medium's almost painful explicitness. It is probably still true that words that might scarcely be remembered when read in novels or heard on the stage can almost never be forgotten when they invade the living room. A now famous example of this occurred on February 19, 1956, when the Alcoa Hour presented Reginald Rose's *Tragedy in a Temporary Town*. One of the actors, Lloyd Bridges, was overcome by the excitement of a particular scene and uttered an expletive that was not in the script but that might have been had the play been performed on the stage. The words themselves would have gone practically unnoticed in a Norman Mailer or Nelson Algren novel. On television, the event was a cause célèbre.

Television writers worked for years within these limitations and produced a substantial body of serious drama, true theater of the masses. They were able to do so for reasons that may be instructive to any who hope to use television to the same end. In the first place, the emphasis was on original drama written by young and largely unknown writers—writers who had little experience in the theater and therefore did not bring to their work the prejudices of theatrical tradition. Along with their equally young directors, they were free to explore the resources of television as a new and unique medium. They wrote television plays, not stage plays or movie scripts. Second, they were not interested in adapting Shakespeare and the rest of the classical canon to the television screen. They wanted to write in the idiom of their own time, and about anxieties and issues that concerned their audiences. Moreover, the young actors they used were not trained in the classical repertoire, and would not have been any good at doing Shakespeare, Molière, Ibsen, Rostand, Shaw, or even Strindberg. But they were well suited to speak in the voices of Americans—a butcher from the Bronx or a bigot from Mississippi or a baseball player from Indiana. Among the actors who got their start by doing fifty-two-minute plays are James Dean, Grace Kelly, Dustin Hoffman, Paul Newman, Eva Marie Saint, Joanne Woodward, Robert Redford, and Rod Steiger. And, since so many plays were required to fill the screen each week, the television networks gathered together what amounted to a repertory company. In other words, there was work, and plenty of it, for writers, with the result that talented people from all over the country flocked to New York with scripts in hand and reasonable prospects of seeing their plays produced on television. As Moss Hart, himself one of America's most famous writers for the stage, once remarked in urging writers to turn their attention to television: "Consider, we write one play [for the stage], it takes months to put it on, and then, if it's a success, we play it eight performances a week, two hours a performance. When we sell out, we reach a weekly audience of perhaps nine thousand people . . . if we sell out." But a television play can be produced in a matter of weeks, he went on, and when it is shown, millions of people see it at once. Of course, many of the plays produced during this period were terrible and quickly forgotten. But that was also the case with Elizabethan drama. We judge an era by its successes, not its failures.

Speaking of failures, perhaps the most important feature of this era was the relative absence of a fear of failure. Plays were not excessively expensive to produce. Thus, failure was not a financial catastrophe, as it is now, and was then in the theater and movies. Moreover, each program was sponsored by only one company, and these were often headed by entrepreneurs who were themselves men of daring, not terrified by failure. Neither were the writers and directors, who were filled with the enthusiasm and conviction of youth. They had something to say and they were not afraid to say it.

Finally, there were the audiences of the time. These audiences were made up of people who were not over-saturated with television. In those days, television was not on twenty-four hours a day, and the screen was not filled with programs that dull the senses. People looked forward to these weekly dramas, and expected them to be serious and thought-provoking. Unlike today, the commercials were not overbearing, and were designed to fit the mood of the play. The play was the thing, not the commercial. And the play invariably was about the experience and world of the audience. Its characters were recognizable, its issues relevant, its language mature and comprehensible, its themes realistic and poignant.

Beginning about 1960, the fifty-two-minute play and its variations began to disappear. There were many reasons for its demise. For one thing, writers discovered that there was much more money to be made writing movie scripts, and many of them fled to Hollywood, including, by the way, Paddy Chayefsky. Some of them left because they objected to the limitations imposed by the television screen, including the commercial interruptions, and they hoped to find greater artistic freedom on the stage and in the movies. Second, and of special importance, was the advent of color, videotape, improved editing techniques, and other technical developments, including the use of film. Television became a technician's medium, not a writer's medium. Everyone became fascinated with the ingenious possibilities of technical magic—which is also the case, by the way, with current American filmmakers—and the quality of scripts came to be irrelevant. Third, television broadcasting began to occupy all the hours of the day, and it is of course impossible to write and produce meaningful drama for such a ravenous consumer of talent and material. Entrepreneurs and executives had discovered that television is a vast, unsleeping money machine, provided that it is used to keep viewers in a condition of almost psychopathic consumership. Thus, American television turned away from serious, provocative, original drama, and toward sit-coms, soap operas, and game shows. In other words, the function of television changed. Its uses fell into the hands of merchants who, obviously, have a different agenda from serious artists.

Now, what relevance does all this have for Swedish television? I don't know enough about your situation to say for sure. But I know a little, and I believe the signs are encouraging. For example, you have audiences that are not yet saturated with television, so they are neither cynical nor stupefied. Your merchants have not yet taken control of television, and you have stringent government regulations to hold them back. You do not have a large and powerful movie industry nor, I should add, advertising industry, to steal away talented directors, writers, and actors. Your entire nation sits within one time zone, which makes live television a practical consideration. And please keep in mind that the "liveness" of television broadcasts gives them an immediacy and simultaneity that film, videotape, and books can never have. To deny television drama this distinctive feature is the equivalent of doing a film without the benefit of editing. Moreover, there is no need to limit yourselves to the fifty-two-minute drama, although one hopes Ingmar Bergman's self-indulgent eleven-hour experiment, *Scenes from a Marriage*, will not be used as a model. Remember: a television play that can be shown, cut or uncut, in a movie theater is probably not much of a television play.

To continue: You do not operate your television system twenty-four hours a day, so television will not eat everyone up in two months. You have a rich culture that is increasingly significant in world affairs, especially in its effort to reduce international paranoia and nuclear-bomb madness. So your writers are provided with weighty themes to explore, and they have the political freedom to do so. At the same time, your culture creates disturbing problems for its people, leading to the development of interesting and serious grievances. Keep in mind that grievance, as Ibsen and Strindberg have shown us, is always the stuff of important drama. And finally, I assume you have a wealth of young and energetic writers and directors who are not obsessed with technological wizardry but who, on the contrary, are passionate about the mystical and transcendent possibilities of the dramatized word. Thus, the conditions are present here for the emergence of a television theater that will speak to and for a national audience who will support and take pride in it.

If I am wrong in this assessment, I hope you will be gentle and circumspect in correcting me. I am trying my best to see things in a positive way, and it is not good for my health to get too much bad news.

Columbusity

As a teacher of long standing, I have had to think deeply on the question, How can I help students to get an idea? Although the matter is almost never discussed by educationists and their critics, the fact is that "getting an idea" is not at all easy, and most students suffer more from an inability to generate ideas than from any other learning deficiency. One of the ways that seem to help is to ask them to survey their stock of beliefs, choose one of them that they hold deeply, and then argue that its opposite is true. The result is often liberating, and provides confirmation of the commonplace that playing with language is an important means of making discoveries. In the following essay, I have used the technique myself.

Serendipity is the word we use when someone who is looking for one thing discovers another, more valuable thing. It is odd that we have no word for serendipity's close-by but troublesome cousin, especially because it is a more common variety of experience. I refer to a situation in which someone looks for one thing, discovers a more valuable thing, but *doesn't know it*. I propose the word "columbusity," in honor of Christopher Columbus, who in looking for

China discovered the New World but persisted in believing he hadn't.

Columbusity visits us all at one time or another, and comes in several disguises. In the case of Columbus, he was afflicted with too much confidence in himself and his beliefs about the size of the world to notice that in his defeat he had achieved a great victory. His columbusity came in the form of *hubris*. But it may also come in the form of fear. We may, for example, be so preoccupied with defending ourselves against attack that we are unable to recognize when our enemy is inadvertently helping our cause. This is why Napoleon warned his generals that they must never interrupt an enemy when he is in the process of committing suicide.

Napoleon's advice is particularly apt for liberal educators who are so unsettled by right-wing assaults that they do not recognize a suicide when they see it. Let us take two examples among several that are available. Perhaps the most serious attack on liberal education in America comes from fundamentalist Christians who wish Creation Science to be taught in the schools. Like evolution, Creation Science purports to explain how the world and all that's in it came to be, but does so by taking the Bible as an infallible account of the world's history. For reasons too complex for me to understand, more and more people believe in Creation Science, and not a few of them have taken the inevitable line that their belief is infused with sufficient respectability to be included in the school curriculum. Among the more articulate of those is George E. Hahn, who has written the following:

> Why do we want to see creation-science in public schools? First, we feel that students have the right to know. At present, few students are exposed to the weaknesses of evolution, let alone to the data supporting the creation-science alternative. Including

creation-science in a balanced approach would keep both positions honest.

"CREATION-SCIENCE AND EDUCATION,"
Phi Delta Kappan (April 1982)

With enemies like Mr. Hahn, liberals and other lovers of science don't need friends. The trouble is that they don't seem to know it. Without considering the implications of Mr. Hahn's challenge, they rush to defend evolution by banishing Creation Science. In doing so, they sound much like those legislators who in 1925 prohibited by law the teaching of evolution in Tennessee. In that case, anti-evolutionists were fearful that a scientific idea would undermine religious belief. In the present case, pro-evolutionists are fearful that a religious idea will undermine scientific belief. The former had insufficient confidence in religion; the latter have insufficient confidence in science.

Good science has nothing to fear from bad science, and by our putting one next to the other, the education of our youth is served exceedingly well. Mr. Hahn is proposing that Creation Science sacrifice itself to further liberal education. It is a generous offer, and only those who are plagued by columbusity will not see it. Thus, I join with Mr. Hahn in proposing that Evolution and Creation Science be presented in schools as alternative theories. Here is why:

In the first place, Darwin's explanation of how evolution happened *is* a theory. So is the updated version of Darwin. Even the "fact" that evolution occurred is based on high levels of inference and supposition. Fossil remains, for example, are sometimes ambiguous in their meaning and have generated diverse interpretations. And there are peculiar gaps in the fossil record, which is something of an enigma if not an embarrassment to evolutionists.

The story told by Creationists is also a theory. That a

theory has its origins in a religious metaphor or belief is irrelevant. Not only was Newton a religious mystic but his conception of the universe as a kind of mechanical clock, constructed and set in motion by God, is about as religious an idea as you can find. What is relevant, to both science and liberal education, is the question, To what extent does a theory meet scientific criteria of validity? The dispute between evolutionists and Creation Scientists offers textbook writers and teachers a wonderful opportunity to provide students with insights into the philosophy and methods of science. After all, what students really need to know is not whether this or that theory is to be believed, but how scientists judge the merit of a theory. Suppose students were taught the criteria of scientific theory evaluation and then were asked to apply these criteria to the two theories in question. Wouldn't such a task qualify as authentic science education?

To take an example: It is fundamental that a theory be stated in such a way that it can (at least in principle) be shown to be false. If there is no possibility of its being refuted, then it falls outside the purview of science. Science has no interest in self-confirming theories. Can Creation Science meet the "refutability" criterion? Does Darwin's theory meet this criterion?

To take another example: Most useful theories invoke unseen forces to explain observable events. But the unseen forces (e.g., gravity) should be capable of generating fairly reliable predictions. Does the invocation of God in Creation Science meet this criterion? Does Natural Selection?

I suspect that when these two theories are put side by side and students are given the freedom to judge their merit as science, Creation theory will fail ignominiously (although Natural Selection is far from faultless). In any case, we must take our chances. It is not only bad science to allow disputes over theory to go unexamined, but also bad education.

Some argue that the schools have neither the time nor the obligation to take notice of every discarded or disreputable scientific theory. "If we carried your logic through," one science professor has said to me, "we would be teaching post-Copernican astronomy alongside Ptolemaic astronomy." Exactly, and for two good reasons. The first was succinctly expressed in an essay George Orwell wrote about George Bernard Shaw's remark that we are more gullible and superstitious today than people were in the Middle Ages. Shaw offered as an example of modern credulity the widespread belief that the earth is round. The average man, Shaw said, cannot advance a single reason for believing this. Orwell took Shaw's remark to heart and examined carefully his own reasons for believing the world to be round. He concluded that Shaw was right, that most of his scientific beliefs rested solely on the authority of scientists. In other words, most students have no idea why Copernicus is to be preferred over Ptolemy. If they know of Ptolemy at all, they know that he was "wrong" and Copernicus was "right," but only because their teacher or textbook says so. This way of believing is what scientists regard as dogmatic and authoritarian. It is the exact opposite of scientific belief. Real science education would ask students to consider with an open mind the Ptolemaic and Copernican world views, array the arguments for and against each, and then explain why they think one is to be preferred over the other.

A second reason to support this approach is that science, like any other subject, is distorted if it is not taught from a historical perspective. Ptolemaic astronomy may be a refuted scientific theory but, for that very reason, it is useful in helping students to see that knowledge is a quest, not a commodity; that what we think we know comes out of what we once thought we knew; and that what we will know in the future may make hash of what we now believe.

Of course, this is not to say that every new or resurrected explanation for the ways of the world should be given serious attention in our schools. Teachers, as always, need to choose—in this case by asking which theories are most valuable in helping students to clarify the bases of their beliefs. Ptolemaic theory, it seems to me, is excellent for this purpose. And so is Creation Science. It makes claims on the minds and emotions of many people; its dominion has lasted for centuries and is thus of great historical interest; and in its modern incarnation it makes an explicit claim to the status of science.

It remains for me to address the point (not quite an argument) that we dare not admit Creation Science as an alternative to Evolution because most science teachers do not know much about the history and philosophy of science, and even less about the rules by which scientific theories are assessed; that is to say, they are not equipped to teach science as anything but dogma. If this is true, then we have made a serendipitous discovery and should take action at once to correct a serious deficiency, i.e., by improving the way science teachers are educated.

A second example of columbusity originates in still another assault by the fertile right wing. This one is not as infamous as Creation Science but nonetheless offers liberal educators an excellent opportunity to improve themselves, their students, and education in general. I refer to the movement known as Accuracy in Academia (AIA), an offshoot of a right-wing group called Accuracy in Media (AIM), which carefully monitors newspapers, radio, and television in an effort to discover left-wing bias. Mr. Reed Irvine, who heads AIM, has now extended his surveillances to include the classroom. The idea is to have members of AIA, who would mostly be students, secretly but carefully monitor the lectures and remarks of their teachers with the purpose of exposing inaccuracies and standard-brand academic opinions, most of which tend to lean toward the port side. Naturally, liberals have reacted with disdain, chagrin, righteousness, and other varieties of defensiveness to the thought of student-spies assiduously evaluating everything their teachers say.

Befogged by columbusity, liberals have overlooked the fact that Reed Irvine has come up with the best idea yet invented for achieving what every teacher—left-wing, right-wing, or center—longs for: first, to get students to pay attention, and second, to get them to think critically. Of course, the flaw in Irvine's idea is that he wishes students to think critically in only one direction. But this is easily corrected. All that is necessary is that at the beginning of each course the teacher address students in the following way:

During this semester, I will be doing a great deal of talking. I will be giving lectures, answering questions, and conducting discussions. Since I am an imperfect scholar and, even more certainly, a fallible human being, I will inevitably be making factual errors, drawing some unjustifiable conclusions, and perhaps passing along my opinions as facts. I should be very unhappy if you were unaware of these mistakes. To minimize that possibility, I am going to make you all honorary members of Accuracy in Academia. Your task is to make sure that none of my errors goes by unnoticed. At the beginning of each class I will, in fact, ask you to reveal whatever errors I made in the previous session. You must, of course, say why these are errors, indicate the source of your authority, and, if possible, suggest a truer or more useful or less biased way of formulating what I said. Your grade in this course will be based to some extent on the rigor with which you pursue my mistakes. And to ensure that you do not fall into the torpor that is so common among students, I will, from time to time, deliberately include some patently untrue statements and some outrageous opinions.

There is no need for you to do this alone. You should consult with your classmates, perhaps even form a study group which can collectively review the things I have said. Nothing would please me more than for one or several of you to ask for class time in which to present a corrected or alternative version of one of my lectures.

It is a good guess that Mr. Irvine did not have this sort of thing in mind. That is unimportant, just as it is unimportant that Columbus thought he was in the East Indies. A discovery is a discovery, and an idea is an idea. Its source is irrelevant. In fact, these days the most advanced liberal ideas seem to come from the right wing. That the right wing doesn't know it is probably understandable. That the liberal wing doesn't is quite unforgivable.

Alfred Korzybski

In 1976, I was appointed editor of ETC: The Journal of
General Semantics. *For ten years, I served in that capacity,
and with each passing year, my respect for Alfred Korzybski increased and my respect for those academics who kept
themselves and their students ignorant of his work de-
creased. I here pay my respects to a unique explorer, and
by implication mean to express my disdain for those language educators who steep their students in irrelevancies
and who believe that William Safire and Edwin Newman
have something important to say about language.*

Because he did not have time to read every new book
in his field, the great Polish anthropologist Bronislaw
Malinowski used a simple and efficient method of deciding which ones were worth his attention: Upon receiving
a new book, he immediately checked the index to see if his
name was cited, and how often. The more "Malinowski,"
the more compelling the book. No "Malinowski," and he
doubted that the subject of the book was anthropology at
all. Considering his role in inventing the field, Malinowski
was more realistic than egotistic, and one can think of half
a dozen twentieth-century scholars who, were they alive

today, would be entitled to employ the same method: Freud, George Herbert Mead, Bertrand Russell, Edward Sapir, John Dewey, Einstein—to name those who come at once to mind. Their names dominate the indexes of books in their fields, and justly so.

The name of Malinowski's countryman Alfred Korzybski, the founder of general semantics, ought to be on this list, but sadly and deplorably is not. I have, for the record, checked the indexes of fifty recent books claiming to be about the subject of language and meaning. Using the Malinowski method, Korzybski would find only four of them worth his attention. The others, he might say, are scarcely about language and meaning at all. This state of affairs—this neglect of the work of one of our century's extraordinary synthesizers—accounts in part for the limited range and depth of the field of semantics as it is practiced today, and almost wholly for its lack of usefulness.

Something needs to be done about this, which is why I hope to hold your attention long enough to recount Korzybski's vast and original contribution to an understanding of the symbolic process, most particularly in his landmark book *Science and Sanity: An Introduction to Non-Aristotelian Systems and General Semantics.*

Except for the fact that he was born in Poland in 1879, not much is known about Korzybski's early years. He claimed to be of royal ancestry and referred to himself as Count Alfred Korzybski, which did not endear him to academics—some of whom used this against him as evidence of the bogusness of his ideas. Nonetheless, from all accounts, Korzybski's bearing *was* distinctly imperial, an effect sharply heightened by his marble-bald head, his accent, and something in his countenance that approximated a sneer of cold command. According to the recollections of those who knew him, the total impression of his physical presence was similar to that conveyed by, say, the later Erich von Stroheim. To complete the picture, Korzybski also had a pronounced limp, a legacy from a wound he received while serving as an artillery officer in World War I.

His wound was not his only legacy from the Great War. The carnage and horror he witnessed left him haunted by a question of singular importance. Korzybski, who was trained in mathematics and engineering, wondered why scientists could have such astonishing successes in discovering the mysteries of nature while, at the same time, the non-scientific community experienced appalling failure in its efforts to solve psychological, social, and political problems. Scientists signify their triumphs by almost daily announcements of new theories, new discoveries, new pathways to knowledge. The rest of us announce our failures by warring against ourselves and others. Korzybski began to publish his answer to this enigma in 1921 in his *Manhood of Humanity: The Science and Art of Human Engineering*. This was followed in 1926 by *Time-Binding: The General Theory,* and finally by his magnum opus, *Science and Sanity,* in 1933.

In formulating his answer, Korzybski was at all times concerned that his ideas should have practical applications. He conceived of himself as an educator who would offer to humanity both a theory and a method by which it might find some release from the poignant yet catastrophic ignorance whose consequences were to be witnessed in all the historic forms of human degradation. This, too, was held against him by many academics, who accused him of grandiosity and *hubris*. Perhaps if Korzybski had thought *smaller*, his name would now appear larger in scholarly indexes.

Of course, the academics were right, from their point of view. Korzybski's thought *was* grandiose in that he took all knowledge to be within his scope. And, one might add, he disdained any tribute to him in which he was classified as a semanticist. Semantics, he repeatedly observed, is the study of the meanings of words. To practice semantics, one does not require knowledge of biology, chemistry, neurology, psychiatry, anthropology, and physics. To practice neuro-linguistics, or neuro-semantics, or, as he finally chose to call his work, general semantics, one does.

Korzybski began his quest to discover the roots of human achievement and failure by identifying a critical functional difference between humans and other forms of life. We are, to use his phrase, "time-binders," while plants are "chemistry-binders," and animals are "space-binders." Chemistry-binding is the capacity to transform sunlight into organic chemical energy; space-binding, the capacity to move about and control a physical environment. Humans have these capacities, too, but are unique in their ability to transport their experience through time. As time-binders, we can accumulate knowledge from the past and communicate what we know to the future. Science-fiction writers need not strain invention in their search for interesting time-transporting machinery: *we* are the universe's time machines.

Our principal means of accomplishing the binding of time is the symbol. But our capacity to symbolize is dependent upon and integral to another process, which Korzybski called "abstracting." Abstracting is the continuous activity of selecting, omitting, and organizing the details of reality so that we experience the world as patterned and coherent. Korzybski shared with Heraclitus the assumption that the world is undergoing continuous change and that no two events are identical. We give stability to our world only through our capacity to re-create it by ignoring differences and attending to similarities: although we know that we cannot step into the "same" river twice, abstracting allows us to act as if we can.

One of Korzybski's most interesting and fundamental

creations was a model of the abstracting process. He actually built a comical, curious-looking mobile which he called the structural differential, whose purpose was to show how our abstracting activity proceeds from lower to higher orders. We abstract at the neurological level, at the physiological level, at the perceptual level, at the verbal level; all of our systems of interaction with the world are engaged in selecting data from the world, organizing data, generalizing data. An abstraction, to put it simply, is a kind of summary of what the world is like, a generalization about its structure.

Korzybski might explain the process in the following way: Let us suppose we are confronted by the phenomenon we call a "cup." We must understand, first of all, that a "cup" is not a thing but an event; modern physics tells us that a cup is made of billions of electrons in constant movement, undergoing continuous change. Although none of this activity is perceptible to us, it is important to acknowledge it because by so doing we may grasp the idea that *the world is not the way we see it*. What we see is a summary—an abstraction, if you will—of electronic activity. But even what we *can* see is not what we *do* see. No one has ever seen a cup in its entirety, all at once in space-time. We see only parts of wholes. But usually we see enough to allow us to reconstruct the whole and to act as if we know what we are dealing with. Sometimes, such a reconstruction betrays us, as when we lift a "cup" to sip our coffee and find that the coffee has settled in our lap rather than on our palate. But most of the time, our assumptions about a "cup" will work, and we carry those assumptions forward in a useful way by the act of naming. Thus we are assisted immeasurably in our evaluations of the world by our language, which provides us with names for the events that confront us, and by naming them tells us what to expect and how to prepare ourselves for action.

The naming of things, of course, is an abstraction of a

very high order (entirely beyond the capacity of animals) and of crucial importance. By naming an event and categorizing it as a "thing," we create a vivid and more or less permanent map of what the world is like. But it is a curious map, indeed. The word "cup," for example, *does not in fact denote anything that actually exists in the world*. It is a concept, a summary of millions of particular things that have a similar look and function. The word "tableware" is at a still higher level of abstraction, since it includes all the things we normally call cups but also millions of things that look nothing like cups but have a vaguely similar function.

The critical point about our mapping of the world through language is that the symbols we use, whether "patriotism" and "love" or "cups" and "spoons," are always at a considerable remove from the reality of the world itself. Although these symbols become part of ourselves—indeed, Korzybski believed they become imbedded in our neurological and perceptual systems—we must never take them completely for granted. As Korzybski once remarked, "Whatever we say something *is*, it is not."

Thus, we may conclude that humans live in two worlds— the world of events and things, and the world of *words* about events and things. In considering the relationship between these two worlds, we must keep in mind that language does much more than construct concepts about the events and things in the world; it tells us what sorts of concepts we ought to construct. For we do not have a name for everything that occurs in the world. Languages differ not only in their names for things but in what things they choose to name. Each language, as Edward Sapir observed, constructs reality differently from all the others.

This, then, is what Korzybski meant by general semantics: the study of the relationship between the world of words and the world of not-words, the study of the territory we call reality and how, through abstracting and symbolizing, we map the territory. In focusing on this problem Korzybski believed he had discovered why scientists are more effective than the rest of us in solving problems. Scientists tend to be more conscious of the abstracting process; more aware of the distortions in their verbal maps; more flexible in altering their symbolic maps to fit the world.

In *Science and Sanity,* Korzybski presents a detailed analysis of what he believed were some of the important differences between the territory of experience and our linguistic maps, particularly the map we call English. The territory is always changing, especially over time, but our words tend to become static: as realities change, our descriptions of realities do not. Moreover, the territory is not a world of "either-or-ness" or, for that matter, of "thingness." Yet our language depicts it as such. The territory never presents itself in all of its detail, whereas our language creates the illusion that our descriptions are complete. Everything in the world is unique but our language forces us into categorical thinking.

The world, in other words, is not an Aristotelian world where things are either A or not-A and where the syllogism reigns supreme. Aristotle's "laws of thought" are rules for the clear, non-contradictory use of language (at least, Indo-European languages) but are not necessarily the best guide to grasping the nature of a process world. A "cup" is a "cup" only so long as we are talking about the word itself. In that case, a "cup" cannot also be a "container." A word is either what it is or not what it is, and cannot be both at the same time. But the thing itself—that is another matter. The thing is not even a thing but a complex process, changing from moment to moment. "It" may be called by many different names simultaneously and without contradiction, depending on the context in which it is experienced and the level of abstraction at which it is symbolized. In such a world, our language cannot even confidently label what is a "cause" and what is an "effect."

Korzybski believed that scientists understand this, which explains why they now map the world almost entirely in the language of mathematics. Mathematics, particularly in its modern forms, has a greater correspondence to the structure of reality than does ordinary language, and, as a consequence, has made possible the development of non-Euclidean, Einsteinian, probabilistic, and indeterminate perspectives. In *Science and Sanity*, Korzybski made a strong plea for a new semantic cartography, which he called non-Aristotelian, and which would be comparable in its impact on the thought of ordinary people to the impact of mathematics on the scientific community. His non-Aristotelian perspective requires that we learn and internalize the most up-to-date assumptions and understandings about the structure of the world: the word, for example, is not the thing; no two events in the world are identical; no one can say everything about an event; things are undergoing continuous change; et cetera.

In order for us to act as if we understand these ideas (they are usually labeled "obvious" by those whose behavior shows the least evidence of their being understood), we must accustom ourselves to new ways of talking about the world, and Korzybski put forward a set of practical modifications of our habitual patterns of speech. He recommended, for example, that we reduce as much as possible our uses of the verb "to be." This verb, employed in about one-third of all English sentences, not only promotes the notion that the map *is* the territory but also encourages a false-to-fact kind of projection. When we say "John is smart," we create the impression that "smartness" is a property of John, that John possesses "smartness." But in fact John's "smartness" exists in the eyes of his beholder. Through a kind of grammatical alchemy, the real subject of this sentence—the person who makes the judgment—has disappeared, and John, who is in fact the object of someone else's evaluation, is made to appear as the main "actor." To help us understand this kind of sentence—to grasp that smartness is not "in" people—Korzybski suggested the frequent use of "to me" phrases, e.g., "It seems to me . . . ," "From my point of view . . . ," "As I see it . . . ," et cetera. He also recommended the frequent use of time-markers, which he called "dating." When we use a name, for example, we should accustom ourselves to affixing a date to it so that we will remember that people and things change over time, e.g., S. I. Hayakawa$_{1951}$, the Supreme Court$_{1975}$, New York University$_{1965}$, and so on. To assist in helping ourselves remember that things with the same name are different, Korzybski recommended that we employ a simple form of indexing, e.g., Roman Catholic$_1$ is not Roman Catholic$_2$, German$_1$ is not German$_2$, and so on. In this way we discourage ourselves from speaking about "all professors" or "all students" or "all cups." Korzybski also recommended that we accustom ourselves to punctuating our assertions about the world with silent "et ceteras," to remind ourselves that we have not said and cannot say everything that could be said. And he proposed a variety of methods to remind ourselves that our verbal maps must undergo periodic evaluation to accommodate changes in reality. Korzybski, it must be stressed, did not have much patience with those who practiced general semantics only at the verbal level. It is entirely possible, he found, to incorporate his recommendations into one's language repertoire in a mechanical way, that is, without altering one's perceptions and evaluations of the world. However, Korzybski believed that by studying general semantics deeply *and* by developing new language habits, we could re-educate our "neuro-semantic" systems and thus reduce social conflict and a variety of psychological disorders.

He believed, in short, that he had pointed the way toward a humane and scientific method of ordinary discourse.

The 1940s and 1950s were the decades of Korzybski's greatest impact, in large measure because of the considerable interpretive gifts of one of his students, S. I. Hayakawa₁₉₄₁. Hayakawa's popularizing book, *Language in Thought and Action,* and his twenty-five-year editorship of the general semantics journal *ETC,* directed hundreds of thousands of people to the study of Korzybski's ideas. In addition, eminent scholars, scientists, and teachers from a variety of disciplines found Korzybski's formulations to be both sound and important, although certainly not beyond criticism. Among them were Wendell Johnson, Irving Lee, J. Samuel Bois, Elwood Murray, Margaret Mead, Ashley Montagu, Aldous Huxley, F. S. C. Northrop, Russell Meyers, Clyde Kluckhohn, and Stuart Chase. During this period, many schools and universities offered courses in general semantics; at one time in the late 1950s, more than one hundred colleges did so, including New York University. I have been unable to verify the exact date but there is suggestive evidence that in the late 1940s, NYU's School of Continuing Education sponsored a seminar given by Korzybski himself. And in Stuart Chase's popular *The Power of Words,* Chase asserts that an NYU School of Education course called "Language and Behavior" was among the first general semantics courses ever given at a major university. That course survives to this day under the title "Language and Human Behavior."

As I noted at the outset, Korzybski's work, at least in its systematic formulation, is largely ignored today by academic linguists, semanticists, psychologists, and anthropologists. The reasons are complex but certainly include the fact that in taking all knowledge as within his competence, Korzybski's reach exceeded his grasp. *Science and Sanity* is filled with unsupportable assertions and not a few errors, some of them extraordinarily naive. This has turned away many specialists to whom precision and caution are more impressive than grandeur of vision. Then, too, Korzybski was much less clear than he thought he was about the kind of enterprise general semantics ought to be. Is it a new science? An educational program? A therapeutic strategy? Like psychoanalysis, general semantics lends itself, too easily, to the predilections and idiosyncrasies of its practitioners, and there has been no firm consensus about the path it should follow. Moreover, general semantics is not easy to fit into conventional academic territories. It is simply too broad in its scope to be contained within a single discipline, for it is part philosophy, part epistemology, part psychology, part linguistics, and several other "parts," all of which when taken together comprise the university curriculum. In a world of specialists, general semantics appears too diffuse, too divergent, too holistic to suit the modern style of academic thought. In a word, to study and teach it is not likely to further one's chances for tenure.

And yet, although Korzybski's name is relatively obscure at the moment, his impact has been felt. Some of his terminology and many of his insights have found their way into semiotics, psycholinguistics, educational psychology, media studies, and, of course, semantics. Many people in the nonacademic world—in business, government, social work, psychotherapy—employ Korzybski's methods with great effectiveness and freely acknowledge their debt to him. But beyond all this, it is indisputable that together with such figures as C. S. Pierce, William James, Ludwig Wittgenstein, and I. A. Richards, Alfred Korzybski helped to heighten our awareness of the role of language in making us what we are *and* in preventing us from becoming what we ought to be but are not yet.

The Disappearance of Childhood

Why are books so long? Do the weighty thoughts of authors require it, or is it the economics of the publishing industry? Suppose there was a severe paper shortage, so that all books were restricted to a maximum length of fifty pages; would it not be possible for authors (at least of nonfiction) to say what they had to say in that space? Perhaps not for all of them. But most of them could, at least after some practice. The possibilities of such a situation are pleasant to contemplate—the cost of books would go down, the number of books we could read would go up. The improvement in the general quality of writing would be significant.

The following two essays represent my attempt to say, in the most economical way, what I had to say in the two books I wrote prior to this one. If you have read those books, these short essays may be ignored. If you have not, you should be able to get my points in the twenty minutes or so it will take to read each of the essays.

The first essay takes the same title as the book which it summarizes, The Disappearance of Childhood. *The second essay, though I call it by another name, is a summary of my book* Amusing Ourselves to Death.

In the next several pages, I am going to put forward a frightening proposition. I am going to argue that our new media environment, with television at its center, is leading to the rapid disappearance of childhood in North America, that childhood probably will not survive to the end of this century, and that such a state of affairs represents a social disaster of the first order. When I have made my argument, I will stop writing, since I know of no solution to the problem. This is not to say that there is no solution; only that my own imaginative reach for solutions goes no further than my grasp of the problem.

Childhood is a social artifact, not a biological category. Our genes contain no clear instructions about who is and who is not a child, and the laws of survival do not require that a distinction be made between the world of the adult and the world of the child. In fact, if we take the word "children" to mean a special class of people somewhere between the ages of seven and, say, seventeen, who require special forms of nurturing and protection, and who are believed to be qualitatively different from adults, then there is ample evidence that children have existed for less than four hundred years. Indeed, if we use the word "children" in the fullest sense in which the average North American understands it, childhood is not much more than 150 years old. To take one small example: the custom of celebrating a child's birthday did not exist in America throughout most of the eighteenth century, and the precise marking of a child's age in any way is a relatively recent cultural tradition, no more than two hundred years old.

To take a more important example: as late as 1890, high schools in the United States enrolled only 7 percent of the fourteen- through seventeen-year-old population. Along with many much younger children, the other 93 percent worked at adult labor, some of them from sunup to sunset in all of our great cities.

But it would be a mistake to confuse social facts with social ideas. The *idea* of childhood is one of the great inventions of the Renaissance, perhaps its most humane one. Along with science, the nation state, and religious freedom, childhood as both a social principle and a psychological condition emerged around the sixteenth century. Up until that time, children as young as six and seven simply were not regarded as fundamentally different from adults. The language of children, their way of dressing, their games, their labor, and their legal rights were the same as adults'.

It was recognized, of course, that children tended to be smaller than adults, but this fact did not confer upon them any special status; there certainly did not exist any special institutions for the nurturing of children. Prior to the sixteenth century, for example, there were no books on child-rearing or, indeed, any books about women in their role as mothers. Children were always included in funeral processions, there being no reason anyone could think of to shield them from death. Neither did it occur to anyone to keep a picture of a child, whether that child lived to adulthood or had died in infancy. Nor are there any references to children's speech or jargon prior to the seventeenth century, after which they are found in abundance. If you have ever seen thirteenth- or fourteenth-century paintings of children, you will have noticed that they are always depicted as small adults. Except for size, they are devoid of any of the physical characteristics we associate with childhood, and they are never shown on canvas alone, isolated from adults. Such paintings are entirely accurate representations of the psychological and social perceptions of children prior to the sixteenth century. Here is how the historian J. H. Plumb puts it: "There was no separate world of childhood. Children shared the same games with adults, the same toys, the same fairy stories. They lived their lives together, never apart. The coarse village festivals depicted by Breughel, showing men and women besotted with drink, groping for each other with unbridled lust, have children eating and drinking with the adults. Even in the soberer pictures of wedding feasts and dances, the children are enjoying themselves alongside their elders, doing the same things."

In *A Distant Mirror,* her marvelous book about the fourteenth century, Barbara Tuchman summed it up this way: "If children survived to age seven, their recognized life began, more or less as miniature adults. Childhood was already over." Now why this was the case is fairly complicated to say. For one thing, as Miss Tuchman indicates, most children did not survive; their mortality rate was extraordinarily high, and it is not until the late fourteenth century that children are even mentioned in wills and testaments—an indication that adults did not expect them to be around very long. Certainly, adults did not have the emotional commitment to children that we accept as normal. Then, too, children were regarded primarily as economic utilities, adults being less interested in the character and intelligence of children than in their capacity for work. But I believe the primary reason for the absence of the idea of childhood is to be found in the communication environment of the medieval world; that is to say, since most people did not know how to read or did not need to know how to read, a child became an adult—a fully participating adult—at the point where he or she learned how to speak. Since all important social transactions involved face-to-face oral communication, full competence to speak and hear—which is usually achieved by age seven—was the dividing line between infancy and adulthood. That is why the Catholic Church designated age seven as the age at which a person can know the difference between right and wrong, the

ment was not exactly merciful; it meant he would have to endure the scarring of his thumbs. But unlike William, he survived because he had pleaded what was called "benefit of clergy," which meant that he could meet the challenge of reading at least one sentence from an English version of the Bible. And *that* ability alone, according to English law in the seventeenth century, was sufficient grounds to exempt him from the gallows. I suspect the reader will agree with me when I say that of all the suggestions about how to motivate people to learn to read, none can match the method of seventeenth-century England. As a matter of fact, of the 203 men convicted of hangable crimes in Norwich in the year 1644, about half of them pleaded "benefit of clergy," which suggests that the English were able to produce, at the very least, the most literate population of felons in history.

But of course that was not the only thing produced. As I implied, childhood was an outgrowth of literacy. And it happened because in less than one hundred years after the invention of the printing press, European culture became a reading culture; which is to say, adulthood was redefined. One could not become an adult unless one knew how to read. To experience God, one had to be able, obviously, to read the Bible. To experience literature, one had to be able to read novels and personal essays, forms of literature that were wholly created by the printing press. Our earliest novelists—for example, Richardson and Defoe—were themselves printers, and Sir Thomas More worked hand in hand with a printer to produce what may be called our first science-fiction novel—his *Utopia*. Of course, to learn science, one had to know how to read, but by the beginning of the seventeenth century, one could read science in the vernacular—that is, in one's own language. Sir Francis Bacon's *The Advancement of Learning*, published in 1605, was the first scientific tract an Englishman could read in English. Alongside

age of reason. That is why children were hanged, along with adults, for stealing or murder. And that is why there was no such thing as elementary education in the Middle Ages, for where biology determines communication competence there is no need for such education. There was no intervening stage between infancy and adulthood because none was needed. Until the middle of the fifteenth century.

At that point an extraordinary event occurred that not only changed the religious, economic, and political face of Europe but created our modern idea of childhood. I am referring, of course, to the invention of the printing press. And because in a few minutes some of you will be thinking that I am claiming too much for the power of television, it is worth my saying now that no one had the slightest idea in 1450 that the printing press would have such powerful effects on our society as it did. When Gutenberg announced that he could manufacture books, as he put it, "without the help of reed, stylus, or pen but by wondrous agreement, proportion, and harmony of punches and types," he did not imagine that his invention would undermine the authority of the Catholic Church. And yet, less than eighty years later, Martin Luther was, in effect, claiming that with the word of God available in every home, Christians did not require the papacy to interpret it for them. Nor did Gutenberg have any idea that his invention would create a new class of people—namely, children.

To get some idea of what reading meant in the two centuries following Gutenberg's invention, consider the case of two men—one by the name of William, the other by the name of Paul. In the year 1605, they attempted to burglarize the house of the Earl of Sussex. They were caught and convicted. Here are the exact words of their sentence as given by the presiding magistrate: "The said William does not read, to be hanged. The said Paul reads, to be scarred." Paul's punish-

all of this, the Europeans rediscovered what Plato had known about learning to read—that it is best done at an early age. Since reading is, among other things, an unconscious reflex as well as an act of recognition, the habit of reading must be formed in that period when the brain is still engaged in the task of acquiring oral language. The adult who learns to read after his or her oral vocabulary is completed rarely if ever becomes a fluent reader.

What this came to mean in the sixteenth century is that the young had to be separated from the rest of the community to be taught how to read; that is, to be taught how to function as adults. Before the printing press, children became adults by learning to *speak,* for which all people are biologically programmed. After the printing press, children had to *earn* adulthood by achieving literacy, for which people are not biologically programmed. This meant that schools had to be created. In the Middle Ages, there was no such thing as primary education. In England, for example, there were thirty-four schools in the entire country in the year 1480. By the year 1660, there were more than 450, one school for every twelve square miles. With the establishment of schools, it was inevitable that the young would come to be viewed as a special class of people whose minds and character were qualitatively different from adults'. Because the school was designed for the preparation of literate adults, the young came to be perceived not as miniature adults but as something quite different—unformed adults. School learning became identified with the special nature of childhood. Childhood, in turn, became defined by school attendance, and the word "schoolboy" became a synonym for the word "child."

We began, in short, to see human development as a series of stages, of which childhood is a bridge between infancy and adulthood. For the past 350 years, we have been developing and refining our concept of childhood; we have been developing and refining institutions for the nurturing of children; and we have conferred upon children a preferred status, reflected in the special ways we expect them to think, talk, dress, play, and learn.

All of this, I believe, is now coming to an end, at least in the United States. And it is coming to an end because our communication environment has been radically altered once again, this time by electronic media, especially television. Television has a transforming power at least equal to that of the printing press and possibly as great as that of the alphabet itself. And it is my contention that with the assistance of other media such as radio, film, and records, television has the power to lead us to childhood's end.

Here is how the transformation is happening. To begin with, television is essentially non-linguistic; it presents information mostly in visual images. Although human speech is heard on television, and sometimes assumes importance, people mostly watch television. And what they watch are rapidly changing visual images—as many as 1,200 different shots every hour. The average length of a shot on network television is 3.5 seconds; the average in a commercial is 2.5 seconds. This requires very little analytic decoding. In America, television-watching is almost wholly a matter of pattern recognition. What I am saying is that the *symbolic form* of television does not require any special instruction or learning. In America, television-viewing begins at about the age of eighteen months, and by thirty-six months children begin to understand and respond to television imagery. They have favorite characters, they sing jingles they hear, and they ask for products they see advertised. There is no need for any preparation or prerequisite training for watching television; it needs no analogue to the McGuffey Reader. Watching television requires no skills and develops no skills. That is why there is no such thing as remedial television-watching. That is also why you are no better today at watching television than you were five years ago, or ten. And that is also why there is no such thing, in reality, as children's programming. Everything is for everybody. So far as symbolic form is concerned, "Dynasty" is as sophisticated or as simple to grasp as "Sesame Street." Unlike books, which vary greatly in syntactical and lexical complexity and which may be scaled according to the ability of the reader, television presents information in a form that is undifferentiated in its accessibility. And that is why adults and children tend to watch the same programs. I might add, in case anyone is thinking that children and adults at least watch at different times, that according to Frank Mankiewicz's book on television, *Remote Control*, approximately 2 million American children watch television every day of the year between 11:30 P.M. and two in the morning.

What I am saying is that television erases the dividing line between childhood and adulthood in two ways: it requires no instruction to grasp its form, and it does not segregate its audience. Therefore, it communicates the same information to everyone, simultaneously, regardless of age, sex, level of education, or previous condition of servitude.

One might say that the main difference between an adult and a child is that the adult knows about certain facets of life—its mysteries, its contradictions, its violence, its tragedies—that are not considered suitable for children to know. As children move toward adulthood, we reveal these secrets to them in ways we believe they are prepared to manage. That is why there is such a thing as children's literature. But television makes this arrangement quite impossible. Because television operates virtually around the clock, it requires a constant supply of novel and interesting information to hold its audience. This means that all adult secrets—social, sexual, physical, and the like—are revealed. Television forces the entire culture to come out of the closet, taps every existing taboo. Incest, divorce, promiscuity, corruption, adultery, sadism—each is now merely a theme for one or another television show. And, of course, in the process, each loses its role as an exclusively adult secret.

Some years ago, while watching a program called the Vidal Sassoon Show (now mercifully defunct), I came across the quintessential example of what I am talking about. Vidal Sassoon is a famous hairdresser whose television show was a mixture of beauty hints, diet information, health suggestions, and popular psychology. As he came to the end of one segment of the show, the theme music came up and Sassoon had just time enough to say, "Don't go away. We'll be back with a marvelous new diet and then a quick look at incest."

Television is relentless in both revealing and trivializing all things private and shameful. The subject matter of the confessional box and the psychiatrist's office is now in the public domain. Indeed, soon enough we and our children will have the opportunity to see commercial television's first experiments with presenting nudity, which will probably not be shocking to anyone, since television commercials have been offering a form of soft-core pornography for years, as for example in designer jeans commercials. And on the subject of commercials—the one million of them that American youth will see in the first twenty years of their lives—they, too, contribute toward opening to youth all of the secrets that once were the province of adults, everything from vaginal sprays to life insurance to the causes of marital conflict. And we must not omit the contributions of news shows, those curious entertainments that daily provide the young with vivid images of adult failure and even madness.

As a consequence of all this, childhood innocence is impossible to sustain, which is why children have disappeared from television. Have you noticed that all the children on television shows are depicted as merely small adults, in the manner of thirteenth- and fourteenth-century paintings? Watch any of the soap operas or family shows or situation comedies, and I think you will see children whose language, dress, sexuality, and interests are not different from those of the adults on the same shows.

And yet, as television begins to render invisible the traditional concept of childhood, it would not be quite accurate to say that it immerses us in an adult world. Rather, it uses the material of the adult world as the basis for projecting a new kind of person altogether. We might call this person the adult-child. For reasons that have partly to do with television's capacity to reach everyone, partly to do with the accessibility of its symbolic form, and partly to do with its commercial base, television promotes as desirable many of the attitudes that we associate with childishness—for example, an obsessive need for immediate gratification, a lack of concern for consequences, an almost promiscuous preoccupation with consumption. Television seems to favor a population that consists of three age groups: on the one end, infancy; on the other, senility; and in between, a group of indeterminate age, where everyone is somewhere between twenty and thirty and remains that way until dotage descends.

In this connection, I recall to mind a television commercial which sells hand lotion. Or perhaps it was for Ivory soap. In it, we are shown a mother and a daughter, and then challenged to tell which is which. I find this to be a revealing piece of sociological evidence, for it tells us that in our culture it is considered desirable that a mother should not look older than her daughter, or that a daughter should not look younger than her mother. Whether this means that childhood is gone or adulthood is gone amounts to the same thing, for if there is no clear concept of what it means to be an adult, there can be no concept of what it means to be a child.

However you wish to describe the transformation taking place, it is clear that the behavior, attitudes, desires, and even physical appearance of adults and children are becoming indistinguishable. There is now virtually no difference, for example, between adults' crimes and children's crimes; and in many states, the punishments are becoming the same. Just for the record: between 1950 and 1985, the increase among the under-fifteen-year-old population in what the FBI calls "serious crime" exceeded 11,000 percent! There is also very little difference in dress. The children's clothing industry has undergone a virtual revolution within the past fifteen years, so that there no longer exists what we once unambiguously recognized as children's clothing. Eleven-year-olds wear three-piece suits to birthday parties, and sixty-one-year-old men wear jeans to birthday parties. Twelve-year-old girls wear high heels, and fifty-two-year-old men wear sneakers. On the streets of New York and Chicago, you can see grown women wearing little white socks and imitation Mary Janes, and, once again, the mini-skirt, that most obvious and embarrassing example of adults imitating the dress of children. To take another case: children's games, once so imaginatively rich and varied and so emphatically inappropriate for adults, are rapidly disappearing. Little League baseball and Peewee football, for example, are not only supervised by adults but are modeled in their organization and emotional style on big-league sports. Junk food, once suited only to the undiscriminating palates and iron stomachs of the young, is now common fare for adults. It has already been forgotten that adults are supposed to have more developed taste in food than children; McDonald's and Burger King commercials show us that this distinction is no longer relevant. The language of children and adults has also been transformed so that, for example, the idea that there may be words that adults ought not to use in the presence of children now seems faintly ridiculous. With television's relentless revelation of all adult secrets, language secrets are difficult to guard, and it is not inconceivable to me that in the near future we shall return to the thirteenth- and fourteenth-century situation in which no words were unfit for a youthful ear.

Of course, with the assistance of modern contraceptives, the sexual appetite of both adults and children can be satisfied without serious restraint and without mature understanding of its meaning. Here, television has played an enormous role, since it not only keeps the entire population in a condition of high sexual excitement but stresses a kind of egalitarianism of sexual fulfillment: sex is transformed into a product available to everyone—let us say, like mouthwash or under-arm deodorant. It remains for me to mention that there has been a growing movement to recast the legal rights of children so that they are more or less the same as adults'. The thrust of this movement, which, for example, is opposed to compulsory schooling, resides in the claim that what has been thought to be a preferred status for children is instead only an oppression that keeps them from fully participating in the society.

In short, our culture is providing fewer reasons and opportunities for childhood. I am not so singleminded as to think that television alone is responsible for this transformation. The decline of the family, the loss of a sense of roots—40 million Americans change residence every year—and the elimination, through technology, of much significance in adult work are other factors. But I believe television creates a communication context that encourages the idea that childhood is neither desirable nor necessary; indeed, that we do not need children.

In talking about childhood's end, I have not, of course, been talking about the physical disappearance of children. But in fact that, too, is happening. Our birth rate in North

America is declining, and has been for a decade, which is why schools are being closed all over the country. And this brings me to the final characteristic of television that needs mentioning. The *idea* of children implies a vision of the future. They are the living messages we send to a time we will not see. But television cannot communicate a sense of the future or, for that matter, a sense of the past. It is a present-centered medium, a speed-of-light medium. Everything we see on television is experienced as happening *now*. The grammar of television has no analogue to the past and future tenses in language. It amplifies the present out of all proportion and transforms the childish need for immediate gratification into a way of life. We end up with what Christopher Lasch calls "the culture of narcissism"—no future, no children, everyone fixed at an age somewhere between twenty and thirty.

As I said at the beginning, I believe that what I have been describing is disastrous—partly because I value the charm, curiosity, malleability, and innocence of childhood, and partly because I believe that human beings need first to be children before they can be grown-ups. Otherwise they remain like television's adult-child all their lives, with no sense of belonging, no capacity for lasting relationships, no respect for limits, and no grasp of the future. But mainly I think it is disastrous because as the television culture obliterates the distinction between child and adult, as it obliterates social secrets, as it undermines concepts of the future and the value of restraint and discipline, we seem destined to be moving back toward a medieval sensibility from which literacy had freed us.

But I do not wish to conclude on such a desperate note. Let me offer, instead, a perspective that may provide some comfort. In the fifth century B.C., Athens was on the verge of transforming itself from an oral culture to a writing culture. But the great Athenian teacher Socrates feared and mocked the written word. As we know, Socrates wrote no books, and were it not for Plato and Xenophon, who did, we would know almost nothing about him. In one of his most enduring conversations, called the *Phaedrus,* Socrates asserts that oral language is the most suitable mode for expressing serious ideas, beautiful poetry, and authentic piety. And he argues that writing will result in undermining the capacity for memorization, the dialectical process, and the concept of privacy. In all these prophecies, he was correct. But what he did not see was what his student Plato did see—namely, that writing would create new and wonderful uses for the intellect. And so Socrates was right, but his vision was limited. Without intending to suggest an insupportable comparison, may I end by saying that although I believe the picture I have drawn is accurate, I sincerely hope my vision, like Socrates', is limited and that the television age may turn out to be a blessing.

But I doubt it.

Future Shlock

Sometime about the middle of 1963, my colleague Charles Weingartner and I delivered in tandem an address to the National Council of Teachers of English. In that address we used the phrase "future shock" as a way of describing the social paralysis induced by rapid technological change. To my knowledge, Weingartner and I were the first people ever to use it in a public forum. Of course, neither Weingartner nor I had the brains to write a book called Future Shock, *and all due credit must go to Alvin Toffler for having recognized a good phrase when one came along.*

I mention this here not to lament lost royalties but to explain why I now feel entitled to subvert the phrase. Having been among the first to trouble the public about future shock, I may be permitted to be among the first to trouble the public about future shlock.

"Future shlock" is the name I give to a cultural condition characterized by the rapid erosion of collective intelligence. Future shlock is the aftermath of future shock. Whereas future shock results in confused, indecisive, and psychically uprooted people, future shlock produces a massive class of mediocre people.

Human intelligence is among the most fragile things in nature. It doesn't take much to distract it, suppress it, or even annihilate it. In this century, we have had some lethal examples of how easily and quickly intelligence can be defeated by any one of its several nemeses: ignorance, superstition, moral fervor, cruelty, cowardice, neglect. In the late 1920s, for example, Germany was, by any measure, the most literate, cultured nation in the world. Its legendary seats of learning attracted scholars from every corner. Its philosophers, social critics, and scientists were of the first rank; its humane traditions an inspiration to less favored nations. But by the mid-1930s—that is, in less than ten years—this cathedral of human reason had been transformed into a cesspool of barbaric irrationality. Many of the most intelligent products of German culture were forced to flee—for example, Einstein, Freud, Karl Jaspers, Thomas Mann, and Stefan Zweig. Even worse, those who remained were either forced to submit their minds to the sovereignty of primitive superstition, or—worse still—willingly did so: Konrad Lorenz, Werner Heisenberg, Martin Heidegger, Gerhardt Hauptmann. On May 10, 1933, a huge bonfire was kindled in Berlin and the books of Marcel Proust, André Gide, Emile Zola, Jack London, Upton Sinclair, and a hundred others were committed to the flames, amid shouts of idiot delight. By 1936, Joseph Paul Goebbels, Germany's Minister of Propaganda, was issuing a proclamation which began with the following words: "Because this year has not brought an improvement in art criticism, I forbid once and for all the continuance of art criticism in its past form, effective as of today." By 1936, there was no one left in Germany who had the brains or courage to object.

Exactly why the Germans banished intelligence is a vast and largely unanswered question. I have never been persuaded that the desperate economic depression that afflicted

Germany in the 1920s adequately explains what happened. To quote Aristotle: Men do not become tyrants in order to keep warm. Neither do they become stupid—at least not *that* stupid. But the matter need not trouble us here. I offer the German case only as the most striking example of the fragility of human intelligence. My focus here is the United States in our own time, and I wish to worry you about the rapid erosion of our own intelligence. If you are confident that such a thing cannot happen, your confidence is misplaced, I believe, but it is understandable.

After all, the United States is one of the few countries in the world founded by intellectuals—men of wide learning, of extraordinary rhetorical powers, of deep faith in reason. And although we have had our moods of anti-intellectualism, few people have been more generous in support of intelligence and learning than Americans. It was the United States that initiated the experiment in mass education that is, even today, the envy of the world. It was America's churches that laid the foundation of our admirable system of higher education; it was the Land-Grant Act of 1862 that made possible our great state universities; and it is to America that scholars and writers have fled when freedom of the intellect became impossible in their own nations. This is why the great historian of American civilization Henry Steele Commager called America "the Empire of Reason." But Commager was referring to the United States of the eighteenth and nineteenth centuries. What term he would use for America today, I cannot say. Yet he has observed, as others have, a change, a precipitous decline in our valuation of intelligence, in our uses of language, in the disciplines of logic and reason, in our capacity to attend to complexity. Perhaps he would agree with me that the Empire of Reason is, in fact, gone, and that the most apt term for America today is the Empire of Shlock.

In any case, this is what I wish to call to your notice: the frightening displacement of serious, intelligent public discourse in American culture by the imagery and triviality of what may be called show business. I do not see the decline of intelligent discourse in America leading to the barbarisms that flourished in Germany, of course. No scholars, I believe, will ever need to flee America. There will be no bonfires to burn books. And I cannot imagine any proclamations forbidding once and for all art criticism, or any other kind of criticism. But this is not a cause for complacency, let alone celebration. A culture does not have to force scholars to flee to render them impotent. A culture does not have to burn books to assure that they will not be read. And a culture does not need a Minister of Propaganda issuing proclamations to silence criticism. There are other ways to achieve stupidity, and it appears that, as in so many other things, there is a distinctly American way.

To explain what I am getting at, I find it helpful to refer to two films, which taken together embody the main lines of my argument. The first film is of recent vintage and is called *The Gods Must Be Crazy*. It is about a tribal people who live in the Kalahari Desert plains of southern Africa, and what happens to their culture when it is invaded by an empty Coca-Cola bottle tossed from the window of a small plane passing overhead. The bottle lands in the middle of the village and is construed by these gentle people to be a gift from the gods, for they not only have never seen a bottle before but have never seen glass either. The people are almost immediately charmed by the gift, and not only because of its novelty. The bottle, it turns out, has multiple uses, chief among them the intriguing music it makes when one blows into it.

But gradually a change takes place in the tribe. The bottle becomes an irresistible preoccupation. Looking at it, holding it, thinking of things to do with it displace other activities once thought essential. But more than this, the Coke bottle is the only thing these people have ever seen of which there is only one of its kind. And so those who do not have it try to get it from the one who does. And the one who does refuses to give it up. Jealousy, greed, and even violence enter the scene, and come very close to destroying the harmony that has characterized their culture for a thousand years. The people begin to love their bottle more than they love themselves, and are saved only when the leader of the tribe, convinced that the gods must be crazy, returns the bottle to the gods by throwing it off the top of a mountain.

The film is great fun and it is also wise, mainly because it is about a subject as relevant to people in Chicago or Los Angeles or New York as it is to those of the Kalahari Desert. It raises two questions of extreme importance to our situation: How does a culture change when new technologies are introduced to it? And is it always desirable for a culture to accommodate itself to the demands of new technologies? The leader of the Kalahari tribe is forced to confront these questions in a way that Americans have refused to do. And because his vision is not obstructed by a belief in what Americans call "technological progress," he is able with minimal discomfort to decide that the songs of the Coke bottle are not so alluring that they are worth admitting envy, egotism, and greed to a serene culture.

The second film relevant to my argument was made in 1967. It is Mel Brooks's first film, *The Producers. The Producers* is a rather raucous comedy that has at its center a painful joke: An unscrupulous theatrical producer has figured out that it is relatively easy to turn a buck by producing a play that fails. All one has to do is induce dozens of backers to invest in the play by promising them exorbitant percentages of its profits. When the play fails, there being no profits to disperse, the producer walks away with thousands of dollars that can never be claimed. Of course, the central problem he must solve is to make sure that his play is a disastrous failure. And so he hits upon an excellent idea: he will take the most tragic and grotesque story of our century—the rise of Adolf Hitler—and make it into a musical.

Because the producer is only a crook and not a fool, he assumes that the stupidity of making a musical on this theme will be immediately grasped by audiences and that they will leave the theater in dumbfounded rage. So he calls his play *Springtime for Hitler,* which is also the name of its most important song. The song begins with the words:

Springtime for Hitler and Germany;
Winter for Poland and France.

The melody is catchy, and when the song is sung it is accompanied by a happy chorus line. (One must understand, of course, that *Springtime for Hitler* is no spoof of Hitler, as was, for example, Charlie Chaplin's *The Great Dictator.* The play is instead a kind of denial of Hitler in song and dance; as if to say, it was all in fun.)

The ending of the movie is predictable. The audience loves the play and leaves the theater humming *Springtime for Hitler.* The musical becomes a great hit. The producer ends up in jail, his joke having turned back on him. But Brooks's point is that the joke is on us. Although the film was made years before a movie actor became President of the United States, Brooks was making a kind of prophecy about that—namely, that the producers of American culture will increasingly turn our history, politics, religion, commerce, and education into forms of entertainment, and that we will become as a result a trivial people, incapable of coping with complexity, ambiguity, uncertainty, perhaps even reality. We will become, in a phrase, a people amused into stupidity.

For those readers who are not inclined to take Mel Brooks

as seriously as I do, let me remind you that the prophecy I attribute here to Brooks was, in fact, made many years before by a more formidable social critic than he. I refer to Aldous Huxley, who wrote *Brave New World* at the time that the modern monuments to intellectual stupidity were taking shape: Nazism in Germany, fascism in Italy, communism in Russia. But Huxley was not concerned in his book with such naked and crude forms of intellectual suicide. He saw beyond them, and mostly, I must add, he saw America. To be more specific, he foresaw that the greatest threat to the intelligence and humane creativity of our culture would not come from Big Brother and Ministries of Propaganda, or gulags and concentration camps. He prophesied, if I may put it this way, that there is tyranny lurking in a Coca-Cola bottle; that we could be ruined not by what we fear and hate but by what we welcome and love, by what we construe to be a gift from the gods.

And in case anyone missed his point in 1932, Huxley wrote *Brave New World Revisited* twenty years later. By then, George Orwell's *1984* had been published, and it was inevitable that Huxley would compare Orwell's book with his own. The difference, he said, is that in Orwell's book people are controlled by inflicting pain. In *Brave New World,* they are controlled by inflicting pleasure.

The Coke bottle that has fallen in our midst is a corporation of dazzling technologies whose forms turn all serious public business into a kind of *Springtime for Hitler* musical. Television is the principal instrument of this disaster, in part because it is the medium Americans most dearly love, and in part because it has become the command center of our culture. Americans turn to television not only for their light entertainment but for their news, their weather, their politics, their religion, their history—all of which may be said to be their serious entertainment. The light entertainment is not the problem. The least dangerous things on television are its junk. What I am talking about is television's preemption of our culture's most serious business. It would be merely banal to say that television presents us with entertaining subject matter. It is quite another thing to say that on television all subject matter is presented as entertaining. And that is how television brings ruin to any intelligent understanding of public affairs.

Political campaigns, for example, are now conducted largely in the form of television commercials. Candidates forgo precision, complexity, substance—in some cases, language itself—for the arts of show business: music, imagery, celebrities, theatrics. Indeed, political figures have become so good at this, and so accustomed to it, that they do television commercials even when they are not campaigning, as, for example, Geraldine Ferraro for Diet Pepsi and former Vice-Presidential candidate William Miller and the late Senator Sam Ervin for American Express. Even worse, political figures appear on variety shows, soap operas, and sit-coms. George McGovern, Ralph Nader, Ed Koch, and Jesse Jackson have all hosted "Saturday Night Live." Henry Kissinger and former President Gerald Ford have done cameo roles on "Dynasty." Tip O'Neill and Governor Michael Dukakis have appeared on "Cheers." Richard Nixon did a short stint on "Laugh-In." The late Senator from Illinois, Everett Dirksen, was on "What's My Line?," a prophetic question if ever there was one. What *is* the line of these people? Or, more precisely, *where* is the line that one ought to be able to draw between politics and entertainment? I would suggest that television has annihilated it.

It is significant, I think, that although our current President, a former Hollywood movie actor, rarely speaks accurately and never precisely, he is known as the Great Communicator; his telegenic charm appears to be his major asset, and that seems to be quite good enough in an entertainment-oriented politics. But lest you think his election to two terms is a mere aberration, I must remind you that, as I write, Charlton Heston is being mentioned as a possible candidate for the Republican nomination in 1988. Should this happen, what alternative would the Democrats have but to nominate Gregory Peck? Two idols of the silver screen going one on one. Could even the fertile imagination of Mel Brooks have foreseen this? Heston giving us intimations of Moses as he accepts the nomination; Peck re-creating the courage of his biblical David as he accepts the challenge of running against a modern Goliath. Heston going on the stump as Michelangelo; Peck countering with Douglas MacArthur. Heston accusing Peck of insanity because of *The Boys from Brazil*. Peck replying with the charge that Heston blew the world up in *Return to Planet of the Apes*. *Springtime for Hitler* could be closer than you think.

But politics is only one arena in which serious language has been displaced by the arts of show business. We have all seen how religion is packaged on television, as a kind of Las Vegas stage show, devoid of ritual, sacrality, and tradition. Today's electronic preachers are in no way like America's evangelicals of the past. Men like Jonathan Edwards, Charles Finney, and George Whiteside were preachers of theological depth, authentic learning, and great expository power. Electronic preachers such as Jimmy Swaggart, Jim Bakker, and Jerry Falwell are merely performers who exploit television's visual power and their own charisma for the greater glory of themselves.

We have also seen "Sesame Street" and other educational shows in which the demands of entertainment take precedence over the rigors of learning. And we well know how American businessmen, working under the assumption that potential customers require amusement rather than facts, use music, dance, comedy, cartoons, and celebrities to sell their products.

Even our daily news, which for most Americans means television news, is packaged as a kind of show, featuring handsome news readers, exciting music, and dynamic film footage. Most especially, film footage. When there is no film footage, there is no story. Stranger still, commercials may appear anywhere in a news story—before, after, or in the middle. This reduces all events to trivialities, sources of public entertainment and little more. After all, how serious can a bombing in Lebanon be if it is shown to us prefaced by a happy United Airlines commercial and summarized by a Calvin Klein jeans commercial? Indeed, television newscasters have added to our grammar a new part of speech—what may be called the "Now . . . this" conjunction, a conjunction that does not connect two things but disconnects them. When newscasters say, "Now . . . this," they mean to indicate that what you have just heard or seen has no relevance to what you are about to hear or see. There is no murder so brutal, no political blunder so costly, no bombing so devastating that it cannot be erased from our minds by a newscaster saying, "Now . . . this." He means that you have thought long enough on the matter (let us say, for forty seconds) and you must now give your attention to a commercial. Such a situation is not "the news." It is merely a daily version of *Springtime for Hitler,* and in my opinion accounts for the fact that Americans are among the most ill-informed people in the world. To be sure, we know *of* many things; but we know *about* very little.

To provide some verification of this, I conducted a survey a few years back on the subject of the Iranian hostage crisis. I chose this subject because it was alluded to on television *every day for more than a year.* I did not ask my subjects for their opinions about the hostage situation. I am not interested in opinion polls; I am interested in knowledge polls. The questions I asked were simple and did not require deep knowledge. For example, Where is Iran? What language do the Iranians speak? Where did the Shah come from? What religion do the Iranians practice, and what are its basic tenets? What does "Ayatollah" mean? I found that almost everybody knew practically nothing about Iran. And those who did know something said they had learned it from *Newsweek* or *Time* or *The New York Times*. Television, in other words, is not the great information machine. It is the great disinformation machine. A most nerve-wracking confirmation of this came some time ago during an interview with the producer and the writer of the TV mini-series *Peter the Great*. Defending the historical inaccuracies in the drama—which included a fabricated meeting between Peter and Sir Isaac Newton—the producer said that no one would watch a dry, historically faithful biography. The writer added that it is better for audiences to learn something that is untrue, if it is entertaining, than not to learn anything at all. And just to put some icing on the cake, the actor who played Peter, Maximilian Schell, remarked that he does not believe in historical truth and therefore sees no reason to pursue it.

I do not mean to say that the trivialization of American public discourse is all accomplished on television. Rather, television is the paradigm for all our attempts at public communication. It conditions our minds to apprehend the world through fragmented pictures and forces other media to orient themselves in that direction. You know the standard question we put to people who have difficulty understanding even simple language: we ask them impatiently, "Do I have to draw a picture for you?" Well, it appears that, like it or not, our culture will draw pictures for us, will explain the world to us in pictures. As a medium for conducting public business, language has receded in importance; it has been moved to the periphery of culture and has been replaced at the center by the entertaining visual image.

Please understand that I am making no criticism of the visual arts in general. That criticism is made by God, not by me. You will remember that in His Second Commandment, God explicitly states that "Thou shalt not make unto thee any graven image, nor any likeness of anything that is in Heaven above, or that is in the earth beneath, or the waters beneath the earth." I have always felt that God was taking a rather extreme position on this, as is His way. As for myself, I am arguing from the standpoint of a symbolic relativist. Forms of communication are neither good nor bad in themselves. They become good or bad depending on their relationship to other symbols and on the functions they are made to serve within a social order. When a culture becomes overloaded with pictures; when logic and rhetoric lose their binding authority; when historical truth becomes irrelevant; when the spoken or written word is distrusted or makes demands on our attention that we are incapable of giving; when our politics, history, education, religion, public information, and commerce are expressed largely in visual imagery rather than words, then a culture is in serious jeopardy.

Neither do I make a complaint against entertainment. As an old song has it, life is not a highway strewn with flowers. The sight of a few blossoms here and there may make our journey a trifle more endurable. But in America, the least amusing people are our professional entertainers. In our present situation, our preachers, entrepreneurs, politicians, teachers, and journalists are committed to entertaining us through media that do not lend themselves to serious, complex discourse. But these producers of our culture are not to be blamed. They, like the rest of us, believe in the supremacy of technological progress. It has never occurred to us that the gods might be crazy. And even if it did, there is no mountaintop from which we can return what is dangerous to us.

We would do well to keep in mind that there are two ways in which the spirit of a culture may be degraded. In the first—the Orwellian—culture becomes a prison. This was the way of the Nazis, and it appears to be the way of the Russians. In the second—the Huxleyan—culture becomes a burlesque. This appears to be the way of the Americans. What Huxley teaches is that in the Age of Advanced Technology, spiritual devastation is more likely to come from an enemy with a smiling countenance than from one whose face exudes suspicion and hate. In the Huxleyan prophecy, Big Brother does not watch us, by his choice; we watch him, by ours. When a culture becomes distracted by trivia; when political and social life are redefined as a perpetual round of entertainments; when public conversation becomes a form of baby talk; when a people become, in short, an audience and their public business a vaudeville act, then—Huxley argued—a nation finds itself at risk and culture-death is a clear possibility. I agree.

Safe-Fail

*The following story will speak for itself, but youthful read-
ers may need to be told that years ago there appeared a
popular novel called* Fail-Safe, *which dealt with the possibility of our accidentally stumbling into nuclear war. That
possibility still exists. But my story fantasizes the opposite—accidentally stumbling into peace—hence its name.*

Although Russell Groves has been quietly returned by
United Nations officials to his native Yarmouth, England, where he presents no further danger to world
stability, the repercussions of his act will be with us for years.
Two American congressmen are even now insisting that there
be an investigation of his and everyone else's motives. The
stock market continues to fluctuate unpredictably, as if to
suggest that where there was one Russell Groves there could
be still another. The Russian ambassador, Belonogov, appears to be finished. The American ambassador, Walters, having already made two nationwide television explanations of
his own actions, is planning a third. Fidel Castro has announced that it will take a very long time indeed before the
Kremlin can regain whatever trust the Cuban people had in
its leadership. Top West German officials have wondered

aloud if the United States has not forfeited its claims on the loyalty of NATO nations.

All of this is, of course, entirely understandable. We came so close to the brink, so perilously close, that one may reasonably ask if we could survive a similar experience. For what it may teach us for the future, here is the Russell Groves Story, as we have been able to piece it together from various sources.

Russell Groves was, until two weeks ago, a quiet, stable, and highly efficient simultaneous translator for the United Nations. He learned his specialty, Slavic languages, not in schools but as a result of spending more than twelve years of his life in Russia and other Slavic-speaking countries. Born in Yarmouth, England, in 1923, Groves was, at the age of eight, taken to Turkey by his austere, widowed father, Dr. Glenville Groves, who served God by doing mission work in strange lands. In Turkey, Dr. Groves met Natasha Homolka, a bulky but pretty Russian widow from Odessa. For reasons not entirely clear and no doubt irrelevant, Dr. Groves and Natasha fell in love, married, and emigrated to Russia, taking young Russell with them. There, Dr. Groves apparently abandoned God, as well as Natasha and Russell; he has not been heard from since.

For ten years, Russell lived with his stepmother, whose affection for him and the Bolsheviks grew contemporaneously but unevenly, Russell falling slightly behind. However, in 1940, at the age of seventeen, Groves left Russia to answer the call of Winston Churchill, who had warned that Englishmen might yet have to ward off the barbarians by fighting in the parlors of English homes. It is known that Natasha died in 1942 of a case of acute appendicitis. For whatever it might mean, she bequeathed her few belongings not to Russell Groves but to the Communist Party. Meanwhile, Groves served with apparent distinction in the Royal Air Force, being officially credited with the possible downing of three German aircraft. After the war, he enrolled at Oxford University, where it is understood that he studied Russian literature, favoring the poetical works of Pushkin.

In 1956, he came to the United States, where he was employed at the United Nations as a Slavic-language interpreter. Until two weeks ago, his work had never given cause for complaint. If there was any reason to cavil, it would have been that he frequently tried to be too precise in his translations. He would, for example, often provide two or three possible English words where one, according to other translators, would have sufficed.

So far as is known, Groves had no strong political opinions and was not associated, even surreptitiously, with any peace movements. A bachelor, he lived on East 38th Street, where, according to his roommate, Donald Flowers, a fellow translator, he spent most of his evenings reading pre-Revolutionary Russian poets. On several occasions, according to Flowers, Groves expressed contempt for the inelegance of Belonogov's prose. But it is also known that Groves was no admirer of what he once described as "Walters's stammering platitudes."

Precisely when Groves decided to act as he did on that fateful March 8 is by no means clear. Groves himself has refused to comment on the matter. Flowers, however, has testified that it most certainly was a last-minute decision, an impulse, perhaps a spontaneous expression of defiance, or boredom, or independence. To say the least, that possibility is unlikely. Groves's translation was too calculatingly destructive not to have been prepared in advance. It is generally agreed that Groves had in fact planned his translation two full days prior to giving it, although there is no evidence to support this belief. At least one co-worker has offered the charitable explanation that the strain of work on the previous day, March 7, might have triggered Groves's irresponsible lapse. Another colleague has offered the somewhat farfetched explanation that Groves was driven by a latent but intense concern for the welfare of Turkey. Both the cause of his aberration and the time of its origination are interesting matters for speculation. But the rest is part of the public record and is not in the least surrounded by mystery.

On March 3, the U.S. Secretary of Defense announced that whereas American missiles in Turkey were judged by experts to be obsolete, the U.S. would replace them, beginning March 6, with the powerful new St. Augustine missiles, named after the famous author of *The City of God*. The Soviet Union, for many years uneasy about American bases in Turkey, first demanded that the U.S. desist; then, as a token expression of its regard for world law, called for a plenary session of the UN to discuss the crisis. Although the Secretary of Defense insisted that the balance of power would not be altered in any tangible way by St. Augustine missiles in Turkey, he welcomed the opportunity, he said, to offer the world any moral, political, or military justifications it required. Besides, he added petulantly, where the U.S. placed its St. Augustine missiles, or, for that matter, its even newer Martin Luther medium-range missiles, was no one's business except the Pentagon's.

The March 7 meeting of the UN was largely occupied by fervent appeals from insignificant delegations for both parties to use restraint. The record shows that Groves's services were required only once that day—thus weakening the "mental strain" theory. At 4:20 P.M., forty minutes before the end of the meeting, he was called upon to translate the rather inane remarks of the delegate from Somaliland, who, for some quixotic reason, chose to speak in Macedonian. Neither the Russian nor the American delegation addressed the world on March 7, and so far as is known, Russell Groves expressed no disappointment over that fact.

On March 8, the irrelevant speeches of delegates from insignificant nations continued unabated until 4:10 P.M. At that time, Aleksandr Belonogov, his face ashen, his eyes more fierce and suspicious than usual, took his place at the rostrum to make what we now know was a short but most spirited and logical announcement. The full text of that statement, in English, follows:

> Mr. President. I wish to inform the distinguished delegate of the United States that, at this very moment, twenty-four divisions of the Soviet Army are massed at the Soviet-Turkish border. There is no need for me to remind the distinguished delegate of the United States, and his countrymen, that this force is equipped with the most destructive weapons that Soviet technology is capable of producing, including, of course, atomic weapons. If the U.S. government does not, within twenty-four hours, remove all of its St. Augustine missiles from Turkey, the Soviet Union intends to do this for them. So that there can be no misunderstanding of my meaning, let me put it this way: Unless the missiles are removed by tomorrow, March 9, the Soviet Army will invade Turkey.

The U.S. delegation was, of course, entirely prepared for this announcement, to which it intended to reply that the St. Augustine missiles were in Turkey to resist precisely such a contingency as Belonogov now described. Of course, as the world knows only too well, Mr. Walters did not have the opportunity to deliver such an exquisite rejoinder because, in fact, Mr. Belonogov's proposal never reached his ears. Russell Groves, possessed by whatever devils take delight in such matters, was responsible for translating Mr. Belonogov's announcement into the earphones of all English-speaking delegates, none of whom know Russian. As the record shows, his translation was, tragically, as follows:

> Mr. President. I wish to inform the distinguished delegate of the United States that the Soviet government fully appreciates the reasons that have prompted the U.S. to install St. Augustine missiles in Turkey. We are all, in these troubled times, frightened and tense, and little disposed to trust our neighbors. The Soviet Union has, itself, frequently been hostile and aggressive because we feared that others might wish to deprive us of our way of life. These fears, we recognize, are largely irrational, and we wish to make an effort to overcome them. Who knows? Perhaps the United States will even help us to do this. Be this as it may, the Soviet Union wishes to announce that on March 25 of this year, all Soviet troops will be removed from Bulgaria, Hungary, and Czechoslovakia.

The American delegation was, of course, thrown into a panic. Amid the general tumult in the hall, American officials frantically exchanged inaudible whispers. The delegate of Somaliland, who knew not only Macedonian but Russian as well, desperately tried to gain the attention of the president, doubtless to point out that Belonogov's meaning had lost a great deal in translation. To the world's subsequent regret and discomfort, the Somali's appeals went unrecognized. The president of the General Assembly felt compelled to offer Mr. Walters the right to reply, in spite of the fact that Walters had not requested the floor. Upon hearing the president invite him to speak, Walters uncertainly maneuvered himself to the rostrum, where, in halting fashion, he informed the president and Mr. Belonogov that, of course, he had no instructions from Washington on how to handle such a turn of events. But he added:

> I am prompted to remark, on my own account, that we are deeply impressed with the pacific statements made by my distinguished colleague from the Soviet Union. I think it is not impossible that should Soviet troops be withdrawn from Bulgaria, Hungary, and Czechoslovakia, American missile bases, not only in Turkey but in European countries as well, would be entirely unnecessary.

Now, of course, it was the Soviet delegation's turn to panic. Belonogov stood up for a moment, as if to say something; then he quietly slumped down in his chair as other Soviet officials looked at each other with a wild surmise. Belonogov then rose again and walked compulsively toward the rostrum, although the record clearly shows he had not been officially invited to take it. Belonogov later confessed he had no precise idea of what he was thinking, except that the Soviet Union had for years considered Bulgaria, Hungary, and Czechoslovakia a burden on its own economy, and had long sought ways of disengaging itself from them as proudly as possible. Belonogov, who had always steadfastly refused to speak English at the United Nations, although he was perfectly capable of doing so, then directly addressed Walters in English, disclosing a charming accent. He said:

> Mr. Ambassador, I need not tell you how refreshing was your response to my stern remarks. I, too, have no instructions from my government, but I am certain that the freedom-loving peoples of the Soviet republics would be overjoyed to exchange peaceful acts with the United States.

Belonogov then returned to his seat, where he was met by a beaming Walters, extending his hand in friendship and peace. Shortly thereafter, perhaps a minute or two, the meeting was adjourned amid continuing tumult, to which the delegate of Somaliland, still trying to gain attention, contributed with his shouts of "Fraud! Lies! Error!"

Five minutes later, the bottom of the New York Stock Exchange buckled. Golden Missile Development, Inc.—makers of St. Augustine missiles—dropped from 56 to 12, rousing its president, Jonathan Lowry, to dispatch a fiercely worded telegram to the White House, charging that the Free World had been sold down the Dnieper River. Two West Coast congressmen with controlling interests in Egalitarian Aircraft, makers of Apostle ICBMs, demanded openly that Walters submit to a sanity test. The Joint Chiefs of Staff called an emergency meeting to discuss the possibility of launching a Polaris missile attack on Russia before it could remove its troops from captive nations. What happened in Moscow can only be surmised since, immediately upon being apprised of the developments in the UN, top Soviet officials dropped an even more impenetrable iron curtain around the Communist bloc. It is, however, generally understood that Albanian military leaders called a meeting to urge that Russia launch its fleet of ICBMs before the U.S. could remove its bases from European countries.

In short, the entire world, poised at the very brink of peace, was gripped by frustration, terror, and near-despair. Ordinary citizens felt, as never before, that sense of individual powerlessness that Kierkegaard and Kafka had described so well. Fortunately, it did not last long enough for the damage to be irreparable. By nightfall, the entire matter was set straight, principally through the efforts of the chief delegate of France, who, having received a correct translation in French, had only briefly lost his diplomatic aplomb. Upon recovering his composure, he lent his vigor and considerable prestige to the efforts of the exhausted delegate of Somaliland, and together they issued a communiqué which informed the world that there was no possibility of a catastrophic peace. Their announcement, written in French, was translated into twenty-eight languages, and was transmitted through every known medium of communication. It read, in English, as follows:

> Through a grievous act of irresponsibility on the part of one man, the remarks of Aleksandr Belonogov at the United Nations were twisted into meaning the opposite of what Mr. Belonogov intended. As a result, a chain reaction of misunderstanding and fear was started, which, even at this moment, threatens the tranquillity of the entire world. Now that the truth is known, we fervently hope that order will be restored as soon as possible. There has never been, nor is there now, even a remote possibility of immediate peace.

Russell Groves, it goes without saying, was taken into custody and, in strict secrecy, interrogated for nine hours in an effort to discover what group or groups he represented. On television, Senator Clark Croker Dettering charged that Groves was a Soviet agent whose extended stay in Odessa had poisoned his mind against the Free World. Producing maps especially constructed for TV, Senator Dettering proved conclusively that Odessa was in Russia, and had been for years. The President of the United States was, as usual, more restrained, but did remark facetiously that Groves could very likely be an official of the National Democratic Executive Committee. More soberly, he assured the American people that no matter what the Russians did in Eastern Europe, St. Augustine missiles would remain in Turkey. Gorbachev, it is known, told his party in a secret meeting that even if the U.S. removed its missiles from Turkey at once, the Soviet Army would still like to take a crack at invading someone.

Russell Groves was discovered to represent no political cause or movement, but only himself. However, an intensive psychiatric examination disclosed that he was suffering from a sufficiently serious case of anemic morbidity to have been theoretically provoked into an act of irresponsibility. The Attorney General of the United States rejected this conclusion, which, if true, immunized Groves against criminal prosecution. He urged that Groves be indicted for incitement to riot and advocating the overthrow of the national defense. However, the President, reminding the nation that Groves was obviously sick, urged tolerance. His will was respected.

Groves, as reported earlier, has now quietly been returned to England and, perhaps because he is under strict surveillance, has refused to comment any further on the entire affair. But all thoughtful men continue to reflect on it and wonder. As Dan Rather, the distinguished television news analyst, said on a CBS documentary entitled "The Treachery of Russell Groves," "If it could happen once, it could happen again no matter how safe we think we are."

My Graduation Speech

*Having sat through two dozen or so graduation speeches,
I have naturally wondered why they are so often so bad.
One reason, of course, is that the speakers are chosen for
their eminence in some field, and not because they are either
competent speakers or gifted writers. Another reason is that
the audience is eager to be done with all ceremony so that
it can proceed to some serious reveling. Thus any speech
longer than, say, fifteen minutes will seem tedious, if not
entirely pointless. There are other reasons as well, including
the difficulty of saying something inspirational without
being banal. Here I try my hand at writing a graduation
speech, and not merely to discover if I can conquer the
form. This is precisely what I would like to say to young
people if I had their attention for a few minutes.*

*If you think my graduation speech is good, I hereby
grant you permission to use it, without further approval
from or credit to me, should you be in an appropriate situation.*

Members of the faculty, parents, guests, and graduates, have no fear. I am well aware that on a day
of such high excitement, what you require, first and

foremost, of any speaker is brevity. I shall not fail you in this respect. There are exactly eighty-five sentences in my speech, four of which you have just heard. It will take me about twelve minutes to speak all of them and I must tell you that such economy was not easy for me to arrange, because I have chosen as my topic the complex subject of your ancestors. Not, of course, your biological ancestors, about whom I know nothing, but your spiritual ancestors, about whom I know a little. To be specific, I want to tell you about two groups of people who lived many years ago but whose influence is still with us. They were very different from each other, representing opposite values and traditions. I think it is appropriate for you to be reminded of them on this day because, sooner than you know, you must align yourself with the spirit of one or the spirit of the other.

The first group lived about 2,500 years ago in the place which we now call Greece, in a city they called Athens. We do not know as much about their origins as we would like. But we do know a great deal about their accomplishments. They were, for example, the first people to develop a complete alphabet, and therefore they became the first truly literate population on earth. They invented the idea of political democracy, which they practiced with a vigor that puts us to shame. They invented what we call philosophy. And they also invented what we call logic and rhetoric. They came very close to inventing what we call science, and one of them—Democritus by name—conceived of the atomic theory of matter 2,300 years before it occurred to any modern scientist. They composed and sang epic poems of unsurpassed beauty and insight. And they wrote and performed plays that, almost three millennia later, still have the power to make audiences laugh and weep. They even invented what, today, we call the Olympics, and among their values none stood higher than that in all things one should strive for excellence. They believed in reason. They believed in beauty. They believed in moderation. And they invented the word and the idea which we know today as ecology.

About 2,000 years ago, the vitality of their culture declined and these people began to disappear. But not what they had created. Their imagination, art, politics, literature, and language spread all over the world so that, today, it is hardly possible to speak on any subject without repeating what some Athenian said on the matter 2,500 years ago.

The second group of people lived in the place we now call Germany, and flourished about 1,700 years ago. We call them the Visigoths, and you may remember that your sixth- or seventh-grade teacher mentioned them. They were spectacularly good horsemen, which is about the only pleasant thing history can say of them. They were marauders—ruthless and brutal. Their language lacked subtlety and depth. Their art was crude and even grotesque. They swept down through Europe destroying everything in their path, and they overran the Roman Empire. There was nothing a Visigoth liked better than to burn a book, desecrate a building, or smash a work of art. From the Visigoths, we have no poetry, no theater, no logic, no science, no humane politics.

Like the Athenians, the Visigoths also disappeared, but not before they had ushered in the period known as the Dark Ages. It took Europe almost a thousand years to recover from the Visigoths.

Now, the point I want to make is that the Athenians and the Visigoths still survive, and they do so through us and the ways in which we conduct our lives. All around us—in this hall, in this community, in our city—there are people whose way of looking at the world reflects the way of the Athenians, and there are people whose way is the way of the Visigoths. I do not mean, of course, that our modern-day Athenians roam abstractedly through the streets reciting poetry and philosophy, or that the modern-day Visigoths are killers. I mean that to be an Athenian or a Visigoth is to organize your life around a set of values. An Athenian is an idea. And a Visigoth is an idea. Let me tell you briefly what these ideas consist of.

To be an Athenian is to hold knowledge and, especially, the quest for knowledge in high esteem. To contemplate, to reason, to experiment, to question—these are, to an Athenian, the most exalted activities a person can perform. To a Visigoth, the quest for knowledge is useless unless it can help you to earn money or to gain power over other people.

To be an Athenian is to cherish language because you believe it to be humankind's most precious gift. In their use of language, Athenians strive for grace, precision, and variety. And they admire those who can achieve such skill. To a Visigoth, one word is as good as another, one sentence indistinguishable from another. A Visigoth's language aspires to nothing higher than the cliché.

To be an Athenian is to understand that the thread which holds civilized society together is thin and vulnerable; therefore, Athenians place great value on tradition, social restraint, and continuity. To an Athenian, bad manners are acts of violence against the social order. The modern Visigoth cares very little about any of this. The Visigoths think of themselves as the center of the universe. Tradition exists for their own convenience, good manners are an affectation and a burden, and history is merely what is in yesterday's newspaper.

To be an Athenian is to take an interest in public affairs and the improvement of public behavior. Indeed, the ancient Athenians had a word for people who did not. The word was *idiotes,* from which we get our word "idiot." A modern Visigoth is interested only in his own affairs and has no sense of the meaning of community.

And, finally, to be an Athenian is to esteem the discipline, skill, and taste that are required to produce enduring art.

Therefore, in approaching a work of art, Athenians prepare their imagination through learning and experience. To a Visigoth, there is no measure of artistic excellence except popularity. What catches the fancy of the multitude is good. No other standard is respected or even acknowledged by the Visigoth.

Now, it must be obvious what all of this has to do with you. Eventually, like the rest of us, you must be on one side or the other. You must be an Athenian or a Visigoth. Of course, it is much harder to be an Athenian, for you must learn how to be one, you must work at being one, whereas we are all, in a way, natural-born Visigoths. That is why there are so many more Visigoths than Athenians. And I must tell you that you do not become an Athenian merely by attending school or accumulating academic degrees. My father-in-law was one of the most committed Athenians I have ever known, and he spent his entire adult life working as a dress cutter on Seventh Avenue in New York City. On the other hand, I know physicians, lawyers, and engineers who are Visigoths of unmistakable persuasion. And I must also tell you, as much in sorrow as in shame, that at some of our great universities, perhaps even this one, there are professors of whom we may fairly say they are closet Visigoths. And yet, you must not doubt for a moment that a school, after all, is essentially an Athenian idea. There is a direct link between the cultural achievements of Athens and what the faculty at this university is all about. I have no difficulty imagining that Plato, Aristotle, or Democritus would be quite at home in our classrooms. A Visigoth would merely scrawl obscenities on the wall.

And so, whether you were aware of it or not, the purpose of your having been at this university was to give you a glimpse of the Athenian way, to interest you in the Athenian way. We cannot know on this day how many of you will choose that way and how many will not. You are young and it is not given to us to see your future. But I will tell you this, with which I will close: I can wish for you no higher compliment than that in the future it will be reported that among your graduating class the Athenians mightily outnumbered the Visigoths.

Thank you, and congratulations.

INDEX

ABOUT THE AUTHOR

NEIL POSTMAN is a critic, communication theorist, and Chair of the Department of Communication Arts at New York University. In 1987 he was given the George Orwell Award for Clarity in Language by The National Council of Teachers of English. In 1989 he received the Distinguished Professor Award at New York University. In the Spring of 1991 he was the Laurence Lombard Visiting Professor of the Press and Public Policy at Harvard University. For ten years he was editor of *Et Cetera, the Journal of General Semantics*. Among his eighteen books are *Teaching as a Subversive Activity* (with Charles Weingartner), *The Disappearance of Childhood*, *Amusing Ourselves to Death*, and, most recently, *Technopoly*.